A-LEVEL
STUDENT GUIDE

AQA

Politics

Government and politics of the USA and comparative politics

Simon Lemieux

Series editor: Eric Magee

HODDER
EDUCATION
AN HACHETTE UK COMPANY

Hodder Education, an Hachette UK company, Blenheim Court, George Street, Banbury, Oxfordshire OX16 5BH

Orders

Bookpoint Ltd, 130 Park Drive, Milton Park, Abingdon, Oxfordshire OX14 4SB

tel: 01235 827720

fax: 01235 400401

e-mail: education@bookpoint.co.uk

Lines are open 9.00 a.m.–5.00 p.m., Monday to Saturday, with a 24-hour message answering service. You can also order through the Hodder Education website: www.hoddereducation.co.uk

This Guide has been written specifically to support students preparing for the AQA A-level Politics examination. The content has been neither approved nor endorsed by AQA and remains the sole responsibility of the author.

Cover photograph: sibgat/123RF

Typeset by Integra Software Services Pvt. Ltd., Pondicherry, India

Printed in Italy

Hachette UK's policy is to use papers that are natural, renewable and recyclable products and made from wood grown in sustainable forests. The logging and manufacturing processes are expected to conform to the environmental regulations of the country of origin.

Contents

Content Guidance

Questions & Answers

■Getting the most from this book

Exam-style questions

Commentary on the questions

Tips on what you need to do to gain full marks, indicated by the icon **e**

Sample student answers

Practise the questions, then look at the student answers that follow.

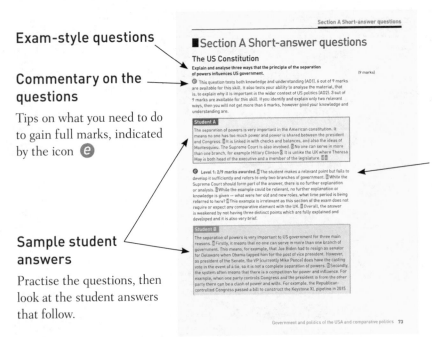

Commentary on sample student answers

Read the comments (preceded by the icon **e**) showing how many marks each answer would be awarded in the exam and exactly where marks are gained or lost.

■ About this book

The aim of this Student Guide is to prepare students for the AQA A-level Paper 2, Government and politics of the USA and comparative politics. This paper comprises a third of the Politics A-level, and all of the topics covered in this guide could be examined in the exam. It is therefore vital that you are familiar and confident with all the material.

The Content Guidance section covers all the topics largely in the order in which they appear on the AQA A-level specification, beginning with 3.2.1.1 (The constitutional framework of US government) and going through to 3.2.1.8 (Civil rights). You are strongly advised to have a copy of the specification to refer to as you go through the topics. The first four topics deal with the principles and government of the USA: the Constitution, the legislature (Congress), the executive (president) and the judiciary (Supreme Court). The remaining topics deal more with how American politics functions in reality: the electoral process and direct democracy, political parties, pressure groups and civil rights. If you look at the specification you will see that a comparison with UK politics is crucial to success in this paper; indeed, the full essay questions are entirely based on a comparison of the two political systems. You should therefore ensure you are already confident about UK politics before you start using the guide. At the end of each topic, there are some comparisons with the UK which should help you when you prepare answers for the comparative essay question. This covers the sections 3.2.2.1–3.2.2.6 in the specification.

You should use the Content Guidance to make sure you are familiar with all the key concepts and terms, and to have a range of relevant examples you can quote in your answers, demonstrating that you are aware of the relative significance of these principles and concepts. Key terms to know and use in relevant answers are highlighted in bold, while definitions are highlighted in green, with the definition given in the margin. Section A questions require you not only to know the facts but also to analyse their significance. These points are highlighted in the Significance sections. You will also need to have a clear picture of how the British and American systems compare for every topic. Make sure you are aware of how they are similar, how they differ and recent trends, e.g. are they becoming more alike or vice versa?

The Questions & Answers section is an opportunity to hone exam technique and to become familiar with the skills and structures that examiners are looking for in the three different parts of the exam. It is not possible to provide sample questions and answers for each section of the exam on every topic, so you need to be aware that any parts of the specification could be tested in any of the three sections of Paper 2. So, for example, just because there is no Section B extract question on political parties in the Questions & Answers section does not mean there will not be one in the exam. The same applies to the short-answer questions in Section A and the Section C comparative essay titles.

This guide does not provide a full range of examples or go into full detail, so you should use it alongside other resources such as class notes, the *US Government and Politics* textbook by Anthony Bennett and articles in *Politics Review* (both published by Hodder Education). You should also use websites such as the BBC or RealClearPolitics to keep up to date with current news.

Content Guidance

■ The constitutional frameworks of US government

If you want to make sense of American politics today, it is vital that you grasp a few basic concepts and facts about the Constitution. It sets out some of the clear principles of government, it says a lot about the different functions of the executive (president), the legislature (Congress) and the judiciary (Supreme Court), and via its amendments it lays out some of the key rights of Americans. The US Constitution is also very important because of the concept of constitutional sovereignty, the ultimate authority of how the USA should work politically: no president, state or law passed by Congress can breach the Constitution. Although Americans often disagree sharply over what it does and does not say, nearly every American of any political persuasion would agree that 'the Constitution matters'.

What are its main principles and characteristics?

The Constitution was drawn up by the Founding Fathers at the Constitutional Convention held in Philadelphia in 1787, following an earlier unsuccessful attempt (called the Articles of Confederation) to create a framework for their new nation. This group of 55 delegates included men such as George Washington, Thomas Jefferson, James Madison and Alexander Hamilton. Among the aspects and principles of the Constitution were the following:

Compromise. It aimed to balance and reconcile a number of conflicting issues between the different states. For example, smaller states such as Vermont were given equal representation in the Senate alongside more populated states such as Virginia, while representation in the House of Representatives was decided on the basis of population size.

> **Significance**
>
> As it was a compromise, and the convention involved a lot of heated discussions and different plans being presented, there is still ongoing tension today over the distribution of power and the exact meaning of the Constitution in some areas.

Exam tip

When answering a question about the importance of any aspect of the US Constitution, make sure you mention the notion that it is the sovereign authority in US politics and government.

Republican. If there was one thing that firmly united all its creators, it was that the fledgling state should be a republic, not a monarchy. Its head of state would be a chosen president and not a hereditary monarch. Note, however, that this was not to be a popularly elected leader but one selected by 'electors' from each state.

Codified. The US Constitution is set out in a single document with written amendments, as opposed to, say, the UK Constitution, which is derived from several sources, such as statute law and convention.

Significance

This means the Constitution is often said to be rigid and inflexible, and cannot be easily altered. However, as you will find in the section on amending the Constitution, this is not necessarily always the case.

Separation of powers. The Founding Fathers believed that the powers of each branch should largely be separate; though it is perhaps more accurate to refer to it as 'shared powers but separate personnel' as in reality many powers overlap. For example, Congress has the power to make laws while the executive/president has the separate function of carrying them out. Yet the president must also approve all such laws and can veto those with which he disagrees. Unlike the UK Parliament, though, no member of the executive can simultaneously serve in Congress. For example, when Obama chose Joe Biden as his vice president in 2008, Biden had to give up his Delaware Senate seat. The judiciary alone has the power to decide whether a law or executive action breaks the Constitution. Again, no Supreme Court justice can simultaneously serve in Congress or the executive, e.g. in cabinet.

Representative and accountable government. The Constitution provides for regular fixed-term elections — every four years for the president, every two years for the House of Representatives and (from 1913 due to a constitutional amendment) every six years for the Senate.

Checks and balances. Closely linked in with the point above is the principle that all three of the US branches of government are limited and checked by other branches. Some examples include:

- The president can veto a law passed by Congress.
- Congress can overturn a presidential veto provided there is a two-thirds vote in both houses of Congress (Senate and the House of Representatives).
- Congress contains a check and balance within itself, as both chambers need to pass legislation, so if they do not agree, the bill will not get passed. This contrasts with the UK Parliament where the upper chamber (Lords) can only delay bills (and then only certain ones).
- The Supreme Court, as noted above, can rule a law or presidential action as unconstitutional, which means it is no longer valid.
- Congress can impeach (remove) the president and/or Supreme Court justices.

Exam tip

If you refer to the Electoral College in any answer about the Constitution, mention that a college is not specifically mentioned, only electors.

Knowledge check 1

In what ways is each branch of US government checked by the other two branches?

Significance

Some commentators would argue that the separation of powers and checks and balances enable the USA to enjoy limited government, with no one person or institution having too much power. Most, though, would say it more usually produces gridlock when the president and Congress cannot agree on an issue. This was demonstrated, for example, by the government shutdown in the autumn of 2013 when neither side could agree on the budget.

It is also argued that too much power is given to the unelected Supreme Court, which often has the last word on matters ranging from abortion to campaign finance because of its power to declare actions and laws unconstitutional.

What does the US Constitution say about federalism?

The Founding Fathers were keen to strike a balance between a very strong and powerful (tyrannical?) central or federal government and a system where the individual states were so powerful that the federal government was too weak to do much effectively.

Powers were divided up between the central government and each of the individual states. Some powers were obvious to reserve for the president and Congress: foreign policy, the currency and trade. Indeed, the Tenth Amendment requires that any power that is not given to the federal government is given to the people or the states.

Elsewhere it was more problematic, especially as time went on and the USA expanded westwards, became a major world power and a more diverse and complex society. Slavery, which was a vital factor in the Civil War of 1861–1865, was perhaps the most evident clash: should the existence of slavery be decided on a state-by-state basis (as was the case originally) or was it a national matter?

The general trend starting from FDR's New Deal in the 1930s has been towards a growth in federal government powers at the expense of states' rights. Such expansion has also gone hand in hand with an expansion of federal agencies such as the EPA (Environmental Protection Agency) or the Internal Revenue Service that have a presence and impact across the states.

Significance

The nature of federalism remains important in the USA today. Many important laws are still made at state level, for example the death penalty, gambling laws and local sales taxes. Several Republican presidents such as Reagan and Nixon called for more power to be returned to the individual states. Democrat President Clinton echoed this call in 1996 when he said, 'The era of big (federal) government is over.' Both George W. Bush and Obama saw more of a return to big government projects such as Bush's No Child Left Behind education measure, and the Patriot Bill aimed at tackling the terrorist threat in the aftermath of 9/11. Under President Obama, the 2010 Affordable Care Act (Obamacare) could be seen as another example of this.

Exam tip

When mentioning impeachment as a check on the president and Supreme Court, play down its significance. It has never actually happened successfully, although President Nixon did resign before he would probably have been impeached.

Knowledge check 2

Give three examples of powers that remain with individual states and three that rest with the federal government.

How can the US Constitution be amended both formally and informally?

The framers of the Constitution made it deliberately hard to amend or alter the Constitution. They wanted to create a system of government that was essentially stable and permanent, with some possibility of flexibility. To date there have been only 27 successful formal amendments (including two on prohibition that cancelled each other out) and another 10 which are found in the Bill of Rights (see below), which was passed in 1791 very soon after the Constitution itself was ratified. If you take out a few amendments which are largely technical, such as clarifying the selection procedure for the vice president, you are left with only around a dozen or so amendments of any significance.

The formal procedure for amending the US Constitution

There are two ways in which the Constitution can be amended formally, only one of which has ever been used. The untried method is the constitutional convention where two-thirds of states could call a convention and propose an amendment that would then have to be passed by a three-quarters majority of states.

The other method is where Congress passes a proposed amendment by at least a two-thirds majority in both houses and the amendment then gets ratified by at least 38 (i.e. three-quarters) states within a set time limit as set out in the text of the proposal.

In total, 33 constitutional amendments have been passed by Congress but only 27 have been successfully ratified by the states.

The most recent constitutional amendment to fail was that concerning giving Washington DC voting representatives in Congress. Narrowly passed by Congress in 1978, it ran out of ratification time in 1985, with only 16 states ratifying it. The most famous constitutional amendment to fail to get ratified by 38 states was the Equal Rights Amendment, which would have made gender equality a constitutional right. Passed originally back in 1972, it expired in 1982.

> **Knowledge check 3**
>
> Why was formal amendment of the Constitution made so difficult?

Examples of important formal amendments (other than the Bill of Rights)

Thirteenth Amendment (1865) — ended slavery across all of the USA.

Nineteenth Amendment (1920) — gave women the right to vote.

Twenty-second Amendment (1951) — prevented the president from serving for more than two full terms.

Informal amendment of the US Constitution

Because the process of formal ratification is so tricky, in reality most of the changes to the Constitution have come through informal amendment. In essence, this involves the president and/or Congress passing new laws or policies that are subsequently upheld by the Supreme Court. In this way, the US Constitution has been able to evolve over time to reflect a changing society and shifting outlooks.

For example, the US Constitution says nothing specifically about the death penalty, referring only to banning 'cruel and unusual punishment'. This has been interpreted by the Supreme Court via various rulings as meaning that the death penalty in itself is not unconstitutional but that it can be used only on those aged 18 or over (*Roper* v *Simmons* 2005) and those without a mental health issue (*Atkins* v *Virginia* 2002).

Significance

The ability to interpret the Constitution in different ways has enabled it to be amended and updated to take account of changing circumstances and cultural perspectives without needing the passage of formal constitutional amendments. Critics would argue that as the ultimate arbiter of these interpretations is the Supreme Court, this gives too much power to an unelected body of nine justices.

Knowledge check 4

Why is informal amendment of the Constitution so significant?

Is the US Constitution a help or hindrance to the functioning of US government and politics today?

Having looked at the basic nature and structure of the US Constitution, it is important to have a clear grasp of its benefits and drawbacks. Pretty much everyone agrees that it is vital to how US government and politics functions today, but the debate is over whether it is a positive or negative force. In essence, you need to decide whether or not a constitution from the eighteenth century is fit for purpose in the diverse global power that is the USA in the twenty-first century.

Advantages of the Constitution

In practice, the Constitution is remarkably flexible and adapts with the times, thanks in part to informal amendment. It has thus embraced the rise of black civil rights, feminism and gay rights. America has become a world superpower with the biggest economy on Earth. The USA has flourished under its articles and amendments. It works!

It avoids too much power being concentrated in any one institution: no president can act as a dictator and must work with Congress to get things done. Equally, Congress must respect the president's views — he is no mere figurehead. Power is healthily diluted by being shared; it **encourages compromise and cooperation**, especially if different parties control Congress and the White House.

Above all, in the Bill of Rights it safeguards the basic rights and freedoms of American citizens, such as free speech (First Amendment), the right to a fair trial and freedom from racial discrimination.

Criticisms of the Constitution

However, the Constitution is an 'invitation to struggle' as the presidency and Congress are often controlled by different parties which refuse to cooperate and compromise. This is known as **divided government** and was the reality between 2012 and 2016, for example, often resulting in **gridlock** when nothing much could be achieved. This inability to reach agreement even led to a temporary government shutdown over the budget in October 2013.

This notion of gridlock has only increased in recent times as the parties have become more polarised and partisan. In addition, not all rights and freedoms are protected equally (see below).

The Constitution contains an indirect method for selecting the president using electors. This sometimes means, as in 2000 and 2016, that the candidate who wins the popular vote can lose in the Electoral College.

The requirement for biennial elections to the House of Representatives results in constant campaigning and leaves congressmen too little time to actually focus on making and debating laws.

Some of the Constitution's wording is vague and subjective: what constitutes 'cruel and unusual punishment', for example? Where there is debate about the true meaning of clauses in the Constitution, it is the unelected Supreme Court that has the final say. In addition, some powers are overlapping. For example, the president is commander-in-chief of the armed forces but only Congress has the power to declare war or make peace.

How well does the US Constitution protect citizens' civil rights and freedoms?

Most of the constitutional protections for individual freedoms are found in the 1791 Bill of Rights. Such rights are said to be inalienable and entrenched. Some of the key rights protected include:

- freedom of political expression (First Amendment)
- right to bear arms (Second Amendment)
- right to trial by jury (Seventh Amendment)
- equal protection clause, i.e. everyone should be protected equally by the law (Fourteenth Amendment)

Critics would say, however, that there are serious problems with the current constitutional protection of citizens' rights, namely:

- Rights are protected unequally. Gun owners, for example, have constitutional rights but women and the disabled do not.
- At various times the Constitution has failed properly to protect the rights of certain minorities. For example, racial segregation was permitted until the 1950s.
- The real guarantor of civil rights is Congress, which has passed laws to expand their provision — for example, the 1990 Americans with Disabilities Act, and the Supreme Court via landmark judgements in areas such as abortion and gay rights.
- Some of the interpretations, e.g. of the First Amendment, have been rather perverse. Should corporations have First Amendment rights to political expression? The Supreme Court in its infamous 2010 *Citizens United* ruling thought that they did.

> **Exam tip**
>
> When evaluating the quality of protection of civil rights and freedoms, make sure you address the matter of 'whose rights' and also have a balanced response. Some rights are well protected thanks to Supreme Court rulings, others less so. Also note how protection changes over time and in part reflects the make-up of the Supreme Court whose job it is to rule on such matters.

How does the US Constitution compare and contrast with the UK Constitution?

There are both differences and similarities between the UK and US constitutions, but arguably the gap between them has narrowed somewhat in recent years.

Differences

The US Constitution is **codified**, while the British Constitution is **uncodified** and found in various sources such as statute and common law, the royal prerogative and convention.

The British Constitution is **unitary**, with power centralised in the Westminster Parliament; the American one is **federal**, with powers shared between Washington and the 50 individual states.

The US Constitution emphasises a **separation of powers**, while that of the UK has a **fusion of powers**. The prime minister has greater scope for an 'elective dictatorship', to quote Lord Hailsham. The British government is formed entirely out of the legislature; in America this is impossible.

The UK has a **parliamentary system of government** where Parliament is sovereign, while the USA has a presidential system but the Constitution is sovereign.

> **Exam tip**
>
> Where possible and appropriate, try to use proper political terms/vocabulary in your answer, words such as those highlighted in bold.

Similarities

Both constitutions provide for and enable **representative, accountable and democratically elected** governments.

Both contain elements of convention which are not formally set out in their respective constitutions. For example, even in the codified US version, the Supreme Court's power of **judicial review** is not mentioned.

The passage of the **Human Rights Act** by the UK Parliament in 1998 has arguably transferred some protection of British citizens' rights to judicial bodies such as the UK Supreme Court and away from Parliament. Parliament cannot pass laws that infringe such rights without first repealing the Act.

The experience of the coalition government in the UK from 2010 to 2015, and the slim majority of Theresa May's Conservative government after the 2015 election, both suggest that recent UK prime ministers have had to compromise and cooperate more with the legislature. Their power has been checked considerably more than earlier British premiers such as Blair and Thatcher. By contrast, President Trump had a relatively strong position, at least on paper, after the 2016 American election, with clear majorities in both houses of Congress enabling at least two years of '**united government**'.

The growth of devolved assemblies such as the Scottish Parliament and the Welsh Assembly has weakened the traditional unitary nature of UK government. Many decisions in key areas such as education are now taken in Cardiff and Edinburgh as well as at Westminster.

> **Exam tip**
>
> When you are comparing the two constitutions in an essay, it is better to argue your case thematically rather than listing all the similarities and differences of one followed by the other. For example, you could start with the theme of structure and discuss unitary versus federal, then move on to consider codified versus uncodified.

Summary

By the end of this section, you should know and understand:

■ The main principles of the US Constitution, including constitutional sovereignty, the separation of powers and federalism, and how each branch of government can limit the powers of the other branches.

■ The significance of the Constitution for contemporary US politics and government.

■ The federal nature of the USA — how power is divided between federal government in Washington DC and the states.

■ How the Constitution can be amended both formally and informally, and why informal amendment is usually the norm nowadays due to the complexities of formal amendment.

■ The advantages and disadvantages of the US Constitution.

■ How well the Constitution protects the civil liberties and rights of ordinary US citizens.

■ The main similarities and differences between the British and American constitutions.

You should also be aware of some of the ways that the Constitution impacts on other parts of US government and politics. This is known as the **synoptic** element.

■ It means that the legislature and executive can often appear somewhat weak as they can be blocked by the other institution, especially in times of divided government **(The executive and legislative branches of government: president and Congress)**.

■ The method of selecting the president via an electoral college can lead to the 'wrong result' **(The electoral process and direct democracy)**.

■ The process of informal amendment means that the Supreme Court can potentially have a major say over laws and politics and is frequently drawn into party politics **(The judicial branch of government: the Supreme Court)**.

■ The civil rights guaranteed in the Constitution do not necessarily result in full or immediate equality **(Civil rights)**.

■ The legislative branch of government: Congress

What are the main principles behind Congress and its structure?

The Founding Fathers envisaged Congress as probably the most important branch of government. It is not a coincidence that its powers and role are the first to be cited in the Constitution and are also the lengthiest. They saw its chief functions as being representative, legislative and overseeing the executive. From the start it was a **bicameral** institution, with power being largely equal between the two chambers of the Senate and the House of Representatives.

The approval of both houses is necessary for bills to get passed, and with one or two notable exceptions (see below) their roles are complementary rather than distinct. As mentioned in the Constitution section, this in itself ensures that the power of Congress is internally checked. It is also worth noting that until 1913 senators were elected indirectly by state legislatures. Since then, like House members, they have been directly elected by a popular vote in each state.

Bicameral A legislature with two chambers such as Congress and the Westminster Parliament.

A key principle of Congress is that the interests of both small and large states are balanced by virtue of the nature of the composition of each chamber:

- Smaller states in terms of population, such as Wyoming and Rhode Island, are over-represented in the Senate as all states are represented by two senators, irrespective of population.

- Larger states are better represented in the House where the allocation of congressmen is based on population, with every state having at least one representative. Thus, the least populated state, Wyoming, has one congressman (more correctly congresswoman — in 2016 the seat was won by Republican Liz Cheney, daughter of former vice president Dick Cheney) for its population of around 600,000 while the most populated state, California, has 53 House members for a population of 39 million. However, even this formula means that the smallest states are still slightly better represented per head of population compared with the largest.

What are the main powers and functions of Congress?

As mentioned above, these can be summarised as:

- representative
- legislative
- oversight and scrutiny of the president/executive

The representative function

Congress, like Westminster, represents geographical areas, so in that sense its members represent the citizens and key interests from their state or district. For example, legislators from Iowa or Kansas will vigorously defend the interests of farmers and agriculture, while those from Michigan will have a special desire to stand up for the auto industry. All members would also be expected to do their best to help individual citizens in their state/district with any problems emanating from federal government and agencies such as social security and veterans' affairs.

But legislators also represent parties so will largely reflect their party's platform and ethos. A Republican member of Congress would therefore be likely to defend the rights of gun owners and support measures designed to protect traditional family values, while a Democrat would normally be keen to support anti-discriminatory legislation and tighter environmental controls. Nevertheless, these are only guidelines, and as you will see in the section on parties, the diversity of America means the parties remain fairly broad coalitions.

There is also a growing case to be made that legislators must take seriously the views of their 'party core', the sort of supporters who are most likely to vote in primaries to select the candidates for each party. As the majority of states/districts are considered 'safe' for one party or the other, arguably the fear of being '**primaried**' is greater than that of being defeated by the other party in the congressional election.

> **Knowledge check 5**
> What is the difference between how members of the Senate and the House of Representatives are allocated per state?

> **Primaried** A term to describe an incumbent being challenged for their party's nomination by another candidate from the same party. One casualty of this was House majority leader Eric Cantor, who lost a primary challenge in 2014 to a more conservative Republican candidate in his Virginia district.

Significance

The different groups that a legislator represents inevitably impact on how they vote in Congress. While party ties and loyalties are undoubtedly important, in the end most members of Congress understand that 'all politics is local' and will put the immediate concerns and interests of their own voters and core supporters first.

The legislative function

This is perhaps the best-known function of Congress. Bills must be introduced, debated and go through committees in both chambers before they can be sent to the president for his signature (or veto). The vast majority of bills never make it past the committee stage, with a typical Congress seeing anything between 10,000 and 14,000 bills introduced and only 3–5% making it into law. Nonetheless, Congress has had a major role in shaping America's history and politics. Among just a few of the numerous important laws passed are:

- Voting Rights Act (1965) — this act sought to end racial discrimination in voting.
- American Recovery and Reinvestment Act 2009 (ARRA) — this measure sought to stimulate the economy in the aftermath of the 2008 banking crisis and subsequent recession.
- Patient Protection and Affordable Care Act 2010 (PPACA) — this law brought in Obamacare.
- Justice Against Sponsors of Terrorism Act 2016 (JASTA) — this law made it easier for US nationals to sue foreign governments if they were harmed by that country's support for terrorism. NB: this act was one of nine vetoed by President Obama between 2009 and 2017 but the only one where his veto was overturned. So it is also a good example to cite when considering the limits of presidential power in the next section.

Federal law always has supremacy over state law, so although **federalism** ensures that state legislatures are key players in the legislative process, Congress always has the final say if it so chooses.

While all federal legislation must pass through Congress, increasingly Congress is passing fewer pieces of legislation. The least productive Congress in the past 40 years was the 113th (2013–14), which passed just 61 pieces of major legislation, though the 114th (2015–16) managed to pass 87 measures. By contrast, the 106th Congress (1999–2000) passed 137 major laws. There are a number of reasons given for this, including the growing complexity and length of bills and the growing partisanship in Congress, which means the opposing party can often talk out a bill, especially in the Senate, a procedure known as a **filibuster**.

Exam tip

If answering a question on the importance or significance of Congress's legislative function, you should note that congressional legislation is not the only influence on US politics and policy making. As we will see in later sections, Supreme Court decisions and presidential actions are also vital in these areas.

Knowledge check 6

Why has Congress passed fewer laws in recent years?

Filibuster A tactic designed to deliberately slow down the passage of bills or to raise a deliberate point by frustrating other business of the Senate. It can involve senators reading out of telephone directories or recipe books. For example, Democrat senator Chris Murphy filibustered for 15 hours in June 2016 to promote the cause of gun control.

Significance

Congress's law-making powers are among its most important but are arguably less central than they once were. When Congress (or one half of it) is controlled by the other party to that of the president, it is often very hard to get laws passed. Congress is under no obligation to pass laws requested by the president, and equally a president can veto laws passed by Congress. This means that deadlock often ensues, and also that presidents will normally seek to get key parts of their legislative agenda passed in their first two years in office, often in the first 100 days 'honeymoon period'. This was the case, for example, with Obama and the Affordable Care Act, where the initial bill was being debated by Congress within months of his election victory.

The oversight function

Another key function of Congress is to check and supervise the executive. It does this mainly via committees that can carry out investigations into the actions of the president and federal agencies. These committees can summon witnesses to appear before hearings and question them. They then publish reports containing recommendations and points for future action. Among famous congressional investigations are:

- Watergate in the 1970s
- Whitewater in the 1990s
- the Gulf Wars
- alleged Russian hacking activities following the 2016 presidential election

It is worth noting that unlike Westminster and PMQs, members of US administrations are not subjected to routine weekly questioning by Congress.

Significance

The scrutiny powers of Congress are a good example of how one branch checks another, although in reality many would argue that given the partisan nature of Congress it works less objectively in practice. For example, Republican-controlled Congresses were thought to have given George W. Bush an easy time over US foreign policy and intervention in Iraq and Afghanistan. By contrast, the Democrat-controlled 110th Congress gave his officials a pretty hard time, partly some felt to embarrass the president and his advisers. For example, criticism in a Democrat-controlled Congress of Bush Jr's Attorney-General Alberto Gonzales played a major part in his resignation in 2007.

Exam tip

If mentioning impeachment as a power of Congress, explain that in reality it is actually one of Congress's lesser powers due to the supermajorities required in both chambers.

The 'nuclear option' with oversight is the removal or **impeachment** of a president or his officials. For this to happen, a simple majority of the House must first vote to proceed with impeachment. The trial must then be heard by the Senate and a supermajority (two-thirds) is required to convict. The closest a modern president has come to being impeached was Bill Clinton in 1998 on charges of perjury, but the Senate failed to convict.

In the Senate, another method of oversight and scrutiny is its exclusive 'advice and consent' powers. This means that nearly all important nominations made by presidents must be discussed and voted upon in both the relevant Senate committee and the full Senate. The highest profile are Supreme Court nominations and subsequent votes. In addition, all foreign treaties must be approved by a two-thirds vote in the Senate.

The power of the purse

Probably one of the most important powers of Congress, especially the House, is its power over government expenditure and raising taxes, the 'power of the purse'. This is derived from sections in Article 1 of the Constitution. As Elbridge Gerry said at the Constitutional Convention back in 1789, the House 'was more immediately the representatives of the people, and it was a maxim that the people ought to hold the purse-strings'. Only Congress can vote for new taxes and spending, and it also has to approve the annual budget prepared by the president and his team. This gives Congress a fair amount of leverage with the executive, but can also lead to deadlock.

How is Congress elected and how representative is it of America as a whole?

Both chambers of Congress are elected using the first-past-the-post (FPTP) electoral system; there is no proportional representation. As already mentioned, every state has two senators each, so there are **100 senators**. While senators represent the whole of their state, for the House states are split into **435 single-member districts**, rather like constituencies in the UK. They are numbered rather than given a geographical title and the boundaries are redrawn every ten years following a national census. This process is known as **redistricting** and is often an opportunity for political parties in each state to manipulate district boundaries in a way that most favours their party, a process called gerrymandering.

Under the terms of the Constitution, **senators** are elected for **six-year terms** and **members of the House** for **two years**. The House is re-elected en masse biennially, while the Senate is elected in thirds every two years, the aim being partly to provide for greater potential continuity of membership in the Senate. Congressional elections held between presidential election years are known as **mid-terms**. Incumbents (existing members seeking re-election) enjoy high rates of re-election due to a variety of factors, so a high turnover of members is relatively uncommon. For example, in the 2016 congressional elections, only 2 Senate seats changed hands and just 12 in the House. In 2014, though, 19 House seats were 'flipped', as were 9 Senate seats, including 5 incumbent senators.

Gerrymandering The term applied when one party distorts district boundaries within a state for partisan advantage. It frequently involves creating oddly shaped districts, often to 'pack' one district with voters from the opposing party and spread one's own voters around districts more evenly to maximise the number of winnable districts. A good recent example of a 'successful' gerrymander would be that in North Carolina in 2012.

Significance

The electoral system used means that Congress is dominated by the two main parties (Republican and Democrat) with, as of 2017, no third parties represented and just two independents, both in the Senate. Gerrymandering often means that representation is distorted in favour of one party. For example, in South Carolina in 2016, the Republicans won 86% of the House districts on just 59% of the overall vote. It could therefore be argued that Congress does not represent the political beliefs of all Americans equally. The frequent (biennial) elections to Congress also mean that House members in particular find themselves in a state of constant campaigning, and it depresses election turnout, especially in mid-terms — **voter fatigue**. The large number of uncompetitive seats also contributes to low voter turnout.

How representative is the US Congress?

Aside from the issues of unequal political representation noted above, the profile of Congressmen and women does not reflect that of America as a whole, although it is becoming steadily if slowly more diverse. Among the inequalities in the background of its members are (figures are drawn from the 115th Congress elected in November 2016):

- gender: 19% women (compared with 51% of the US population as a whole)
- race: 7% Hispanic and 9% African-American (compared with 14% and 12% respectively of the US population as a whole)
- religion: 7% non-Christian (Jewish, Muslim, Hindu and Buddhist) — note that although around 20% of Americans identify as 'No religion', there are hardly any members of Congress who would openly identify as such
- sexuality: there are only seven LGBT members of Congress

In addition, members of both houses are older, wealthier and hold higher educational qualifications than your average American. But while Congress still does not look like America, it is steadily changing. Although the Democrats are clearly the more diverse of the two parties, there are growing numbers of ethnic minorities among the Republican ranks, including Senator Tim Scott (SC) and Congresswoman Mia Love (Utah), who both represent white majority electorates. There were even two gay Republicans (Paul Babeu and Clay Cope) running for congressional office in 2016, though both lost.

Significance

It could be said that having a Congress that is still largely 'white, male and stale' undermines its ability to represent fairly all Americans. Others would counter by saying that progress is being made towards greater diversity in both parties and that with race, for example, ethnic minorities can still be represented effectively by white congressmen/women and vice versa.

Knowledge check 7

In what ways could the profiles of members of Congress be seen as unrepresentative of America as a whole?

Exam tip

A good example to use is Democrat Steve Cohen, who is white and Jewish but represents (as of 2017) the Tennessee 9th District that is 60% African-American.

How is Congress organised and what role do parties play in its structure?

Parties and **committees** are twin cornerstones of modern congresses. Unlike the UK Parliament, the floor of each chamber is less important; most of the real work is done in committees. As Woodrow Wilson said in 1884, 'Congressional government is committee government. Congress in its committee rooms is Congress at work.' This is because most of its legislative and oversight tasks take place in the **41 standing committees** and hundreds of sub-committees found in both houses. As Professor Vile famously wrote, they are the 'sieve through which all legislation is poured, and what comes out, and how it comes out, is largely in their hands'. It is also where investigative hearings take place. Among some of the key committees are:

- Appropriations (both houses) — oversees funding allocation for bills
- House Rules Committee (House of Representatives only) — allocates which committees discuss which bills and the rules of debate
- Senate Judiciary Committee (holds hearings for Supreme Court nominees)
- Foreign Relations/Affairs (both houses).

The majority party in each house will always have a majority on each committee. Alongside their key role as 'gatekeepers' of bills, committees are also important because:

- their permanence and large support staff enable them to build expertise and knowledge to check the executive
- they often form strong relationships with federal agencies and insider pressure groups, sometimes leading to accusations of creating '**iron triangles**'
- they can force (subpoena) witnesses to appear at committee hearings
- chairing an important congressional committee can often be an important part of career progression for ambitious legislators. It certainly gives them additional power and prestige

Parties in Congress

The two dominant political parties play an increasingly important role in the running of Congress, especially the House. Levels of party loyalty have soared in recent years, with average rates hovering around 90% for both parties in each chamber. There are **far fewer moderate centrists** who are more inclined to switch their votes between parties. The result is a system much more like Westminster, with most votes taking place along party lines. No Republican, for example, voted for Obamacare in 2010. The most liberal/moderate Republican senator is still more conservative than the most conservative Democrat senator. That would not have been the case 20 years ago.

Yet the powers of the party leaders and whips in each chamber are still more limited than those of their counterparts in the UK. As party candidates are selected by voters directly via primary elections and not by local parties, there is little incentive to remove the party whip. In essence, most legislators vote with their party colleagues most of the time not because of the demands from the party leadership but because they (and their voters) share broadly common views. The separation of the legislature from the executive also means that party leaders cannot offer the 'carrot' of government posts to sway wavering members of Congress, as sometimes happens in Britain.

Iron triangle A term used to describe the close relationship between federal agencies, relevant pressure groups and members of the associated congressional committees. These connections are often seen as damaging to the wider national interest as each side collaborates with rather than checks the others, for example to maintain the size and funding of a particular department's budget.

You should also be aware of groups (caucuses) within the parties in Congress. Fiscally conservative Democrats, for example, belong to the Blue Dog Caucus, while the most conservative Republicans can be found in the Freedom Caucus. There are also cross-party caucuses, such as the Congressional Bike Caucus (to promote cycling) or the rather better known and Democrat-dominated Congressional Black Caucus.

How well does Congress perform its functions of law-making, representation and overseeing the executive?

Most of the points have already been referred to in previous sections, but in summary, defenders of Congress would argue:

- all legislation is thoroughly debated and analysed by specialised and highly experienced committees
- the composition of Congress is steadily becoming more diverse
- congressional investigations and Senate confirmation hearings provide an effective check on the executive and can often unmask failings and inefficiencies within government.

Its detractors would comment that:

- the high levels of party unity and partisanship in Congress mean that much scrutiny of the executive is designed to protect or embarrass the 'other side' rather than to work objectively in the interests of good and efficient government
- the makeup of Congress still significantly under-represents key social groups
- Congress is passing fewer laws than previously so is pretty unproductive

One of the more paradoxical aspects of Congress is that its approval ratings have been very low in recent times (often well under 20%) yet incumbent re-election rates remain high. Perhaps the fault lies with everyone else's congressperson!

A comparison of the House with the Senate

Although both houses have equal legislative powers (and equal salaries), the Senate is generally considered the more prestigious and desirable of the two chambers. This is because of the following factors:

- A longer term (six versus two years) means less focus on constant campaigning and fundraising for elections.
- The exclusive power of the Senate in confirming key presidential appointments.
- Greater exclusivity due to its smaller size: 100 versus 435.
- Higher levels of name recognition and a greater state-wide profile.
- More opportunities to sit on and chair committees.
- The Senate is a greater 'talent pool' for executive office. Many presidents and vice presidents such as Obama and Biden have come up from the Senate; hardly any have reached high office directly from the House.

Finally, it is worth noting that while the Senate contains many former congressmen, the House does not contain any former senators.

Yet the House has the 'power of the purse' and chooses the president in the event of no candidate securing a majority in the Electoral College, though this has not happened since 1825.

How powerful is Congress and how does it relate to the president and the Supreme Court?

The power of Congress, as we will see with the president, is somewhat variable, depending in part on circumstances and the political climate. When one party has strong majorities in both chambers and holds the White House, Congress can achieve much that is positive via legislation, although it is also simultaneously less effective at overseeing the executive. When Congress is itself divided and/or another party controls the government, its power is essentially negative for much of the time. It can often be pretty effective at frustrating a president, such as with Obama, who sought unsuccessfully to get Congress to close completely Guantanamo Bay and to pass immigration reform.

The Supreme Court can and does affect laws passed by Congress using its powers of judicial review. For example, efforts to reform campaign finance, such as the 2002 **Bipartisan Campaign Reform Act**, have been weakened by verdicts such as *Citizens United*. In theory, Congress could be pivotal in passing constitutional amendments that would bind both the president and the Court, but as we have seen, it is very difficult to get the supermajorities required and then to win the support of 75% of states.

Knowledge check 9

In what circumstances will Congress be at its most powerful?

Summary

By the end of this section, you should know and understand:

- The main powers of Congress: representative, legislative and oversight.
- How the two houses are elected and how frequently.
- The debate over how fairly and equally Congress represents modern-day America.
- How and why congressional committees are so important.
- Why serving in the Senate is generally seen as preferable to being a House member.
- Why parties are increasingly important in the workings of Congress.
- The arguments over how well Congress does its job.
- How the powers of Congress compare with those of the president and the Supreme Court.

You should also be aware of some of the ways that Congress impacts on other parts of US government and politics. This is known as the **synoptic** element:

- Its power is often shared with the president — cooperation between the two can be productive, while conflict or competition can lead to gridlock **(The executive branch of government: president)**.
- The Supreme Court can rule acts of Congress unconstitutional **(The judicial branch of government: the Supreme Court)**.
- The changes and developments in political parties are also reflected in Congress **(Political parties)**.
- Pressure groups, especially powerful insider ones, can often impact on legislation being debated in Congress **(Pressure groups)**.

■ The executive branch of government: president

From where does the American presidency derive its powers?

As with Congress, the formal powers of the president are enumerated in the Constitution, primarily in **Article 1**. By contrast, the informal powers of the presidency and executive have accrued over time and often reflect changing expectations and priorities in society. For example, as government has grown larger and more complex, so have the roles and scope of executive agencies. Also, as the USA has emerged as a global superpower, so has the significance of the president's role as commander-in-chief of the armed forces. Again as with the powers of Congress, the president must act in accordance with the Constitution as interpreted by the Supreme Court.

Two relevant examples

The specification requires you to know two examples of the sources of presidential power. There are plenty to choose from, but a couple are summarised below.

The president is the **head of the executive** and is charged with 'faithfully executing the laws'. One example of this power in action was in December 2016, when President Obama used an obscure provision of a 1953 law, the Outer Continental Shelf Lands Act, to ban permanently drilling on portions of the ocean floor from Virginia to Maine and along much of Alaska's coast.

As **commander-in-chief**, the president has the power to deploy US forces in combat zones without asking Congress formally to declare war. This was how George W. Bush managed to send US forces into Afghanistan and later Iraq to remove their leaders — the Taliban and Saddam Hussein respectively — in the aftermath of the 9/11 terror attacks.

> **Exam tip**
>
> When discussing the president's executive powers, mention that these can be and often are challenged in the courts. This happened in February 2017 with President Trump's ban on travellers from seven predominantly Muslim countries.

What are the main formal and informal powers of the US president?

The formal powers of the president

It is important to realise that the framers of the Constitution did not envisage a powerful head of state. The formal powers are therefore often quite loose and vague. Until the 1930s, many US presidents were fairly inconspicuous, with obvious exceptions such as Washington and Lincoln, but who now remembers Presidents Franklin Pierce or Chester Arthur? The president's formal powers include:

■ **Chief executive**: only the president can appoint members of the government and heads of federal bodies such as NASA and the CIA, along with diplomatic positions. There is also the requirement that he must 'faithfully execute' the laws of the USA. The president has the power of pardon and draws up the annual budget, which Congress must then approve.

- **Commander-in-chief:** the president is leader of the US armed forces and is responsible (and accountable) for their deployment.
- **Chief diplomat**: the Constitution states that the president has the power to make treaties with foreign powers.
- **Chief 'law unmaker':** the president can veto laws passed by Congress.

Be aware that, as the previous section illustrated, many of these powers require cooperation and assent from Congress, especially the Senate.

The informal or implied powers of the president

These are slightly trickier to list, but are generally agreed to include the following:

- **Chief legislator:** presidents are always elected on the back of a set of promises and policies, as well as vaguer slogans such as making America great again or promising hope and change. Once in power, there is the expectation, at least from their supporters, that these pledges be fulfilled, whether this be building a wall along the Mexican border or extending provision of public healthcare.
- **Leader of the free world:** modern global politics essentially requires the USA to take a lead in world affairs on behalf of western countries, as well as other staunch allies of the USA, such as Israel and Japan; hence the lead taken by recent presidents in the 'war on terror'.
- **Party leader:** although the president is not the official leader of their party, unlike the British prime minister, the president is (increasingly) seen as a party political figure and leader, albeit without many powers of coercion. Presidents cannot assume the complete loyalty of their party's members in Congress — witness Clinton's defeat over healthcare reforms in the 1990s.
- **Communicator in chief:** the president has a high media profile — what they say in media briefings, articles or interviews will be widely reported by the media. Sometimes known as the '**bully pulpit**', the president can use this power to seek to win over public and/or political opinion. Success is certainly not guaranteed, however.
- **'First-responder in chief':** in times of national emergency such as the 9/11 terror attacks or hurricanes Sandy and Katrina, the president is expected to give a lead, appear in control and exude determination, compassion and toughness as appropriate.
- **Executive manipulator in chief:** presidents have become adept at bypassing uncooperative Congresses by making full use of their executive authority. This is often done by making **executive agreements** rather than formal treaties with other countries. This was the approach Obama took in reaching a nuclear deal with Iran and partially normalising relations with Cuba. Neither policy would have secured Senate approval. **Executive orders** are another way a president can implement policy unilaterally. President Trump used executive orders at the very start of his presidency to impose stricter immigration controls (extreme vetting) on visitors from some Muslim countries seen to pose a high terrorism threat.
- **Superior access to intelligence and policy resources:** the president benefits from a large bank of policy advisers who are often handpicked, and the resources of knowledge and intelligence from bodies such as the National Security Council and the CIA. With daily top secret intelligence briefings, a president should be much better informed than Congress, and with knowledge comes a certain amount of power. The presidential approval needed to authorise the Navy SEALS raid that

Bully pulpit First coined by President Theodore Roosevelt at the turn of the twentieth century, this term does not mean bullying the public or media into agreeing with them but is rather a first-rate (or bully) opportunity to persuade.

Executive orders Decrees issued by presidents to federal bodies. A couple of examples are those to ban smoking in federal buildings and to raise the minimum wage for federal employees. They cannot be overridden by Congress, but can be and are challenged in the courts.

resulted in bin Laden's death in 2011 was based on CIA intelligence and discussed at a National Security Council (NSC) meeting.

■ **Head of state:** the president assumes the ceremonial duties, such as formally welcoming foreign leaders, that in the UK are undertaken by the monarch.

Significance

All the powers of a president are important, but arguably the informal ones are most significant, often allowing a strong president to bypass a potentially hostile Congress and appeal directly to the nation. Much depends on the circumstances and personality of the individual president. All presidents have equal powers in theory, but in reality some are more powerful than others.

Knowledge check 10

What are the variable factors that affect the powers of the president?

What are the main restrictions on the power of a US president?

The formal restrictions on presidential power

Formal restrictions as found in the Constitution include the following:

■ The presidential veto being overturned by a two-thirds vote in both houses of Congress. This is rare however, due to the supermajority required. Obama had only 1 of his 12 vetoes overturned, while George W. Bush had 4 out of 12 quashed.

■ The Senate refusing to confirm a presidential appointment. Again this is rare: only 9 Cabinet nominees in US history were defeated in Senate votes, although 12 others were withdrawn in the face of strong opposition. The last time a nominee was rejected in a Senate vote was in 1989, when John Tower, President George H. W. Bush's pick for Defense Secretary, lost his confirmation vote 53–47. The last time that had happened before was in 1959.

■ Being impeached by Congress, as attempted with Clinton over the Monica Lewinsky affair. No US President has ever been successfully impeached though Nixon resigned rather than face probable impeachment and removal from office.

■ Having an action declared unconstitutional by the Supreme Court, such as the detention without trial of 'enemy combatants' in *Hamden* v *Rumsfeld* (2006).

■ Congress refusing to pass legislation proposed or asked for by the president, as was the case with gun control measures and immigration reform in the Obama years. In extreme cases, Congress can also refuse to pass the annual budget, which can lead to a temporary shutdown of parts of the federal government, as in 2013.

The informal restrictions on presidential power

Informal restrictions *not* found in the Constitution include the following:

■ A Congress controlled by the other party, a situation Obama faced in his second term. This can seriously undermine attempts to get legislation, especially controversial measures, enacted.

■ Poor approval ratings in the polls. This can reduce a president's power to persuade members of Congress to cooperate. By contrast, cooperating with an unpopular president could affect their own chances of re-election.

Exam tip

Good examples to cite here would be immigration reform and gun control. Faced with a hostile uncooperative Congress, Obama was forced to resort to executive orders to try and achieve some of his objectives in those areas. Such orders, though, will always be more limited than federal law.

- The culture of a 24/7 media makes it harder for the president to respond effectively at all times to criticism and comment. The rise of the more partisan new media, with talk show hosts such as Glenn Beck, also makes it difficult to persuade and influence voters.
- Some (though not all) foreign policy actions require cooperation from America's allies for a president to feel confident about going ahead. The Commons' vote rejecting air strikes on Syria in 2013 is widely held to have dissuaded Obama's administration from going ahead with their own intervention at that time.
- The potential embarrassment of being subject to a judicial investigation comprising a federal prosecutor and a grand jury, as with Clinton and the Whitewater affair in the 1990s.

The relationship between a president and the other parts of the executive

What are the other parts of the executive?

The term refers to all other parts of government other than the president, so among the component parts are:

- **the cabinet** (e.g. posts such as secretary of state and treasury secretary).
- **EXOP** (Executive Office of the President): this is the president's personal bureaucracy. First established for FDR in 1939 to provide administrative and policy support to the president, it is headed by the White House chief of staff — in 2017 John F. Kelly. It contains a number of departments, including the NSC and the Office of Management and Budget, which is the largest section of EXOP.
- **federal agencies:** these include bodies such as NASA and the EPA.

Presidential/executive relations

In theory, relations between a president and his executive should be harmonious and positive, not least because many of the top levels are appointed directly by the president, who normally chooses close aides and allies. In reality, matters are not always so straightforward. There might be rivalry between different factions, a president may choose not to use or consult his cabinet very often (as was the case with Clinton in the 1990s, for example), or a president may face hostility to their agenda from a federal agency which has its own policy preferences.

The relationship depends in part on how well a president knows the inner workings of the federal bureaucracy before assuming office. Bush Senior (1989–1993), for example, as a long-serving member of Congress and former chief of the CIA, might be said to have had an advantage over an inexperienced 'outsider' such as Trump or Obama. The ability to choose close but competent advisers and confidants, along with the political balance and mood in Congress, are also important. Trump's pick of Michael Flynn as national security adviser turned out to be ill advised as Flynn was forced to resign in February 2017 due to accusations that he had misled others in the administration about his Russian contacts. A more 'insider' president might not have shown the same error of judgement in making a controversial choice in the first place. Personal skills and charisma can be vital, too. Nixon, for example, was known for being highly suspicious and rarely trusted or delegated effectively. Reagan, by contrast, was only too happy to delegate, though this had its weaknesses, as shown by the Iran–Contra affair.

The waxing and waning of presidential power

The specification requires you to have **one example** that shows the variation of presidential power within a single presidency. There are many possibilities, including FDR and EXOP, and the relationships of Reagan and Clinton with their congresses. You are free to choose any you like, but the example given here (in summary form) is of JFK and the 1962 Cuban Missile Crisis.

Knowledge check 11

Why might an 'insider' president have an advantage in running an effective administration?

Case study

JFK and the October 1962 Cuban Missile Crisis

The Cuban Missile Crisis represented the closest the Cold War world ever came to World War Three. The communist leader of Cuba, Fidel Castro, had accepted a Russian offer to place nuclear missiles on the island, ostensibly for self-defence, though in reality the missiles had a range that could reach nearly every major US city. It placed the young and newly elected President Kennedy with a dilemma: too soft on Khrushchev's Russia and the USA looked weak and vulnerable, but too harsh or reckless and nuclear holocaust might ensue. It was a classic test of presidential nerve and power.

It highlighted some *weaknesses* in the presidency:
- Poor intelligence from his security advisers and the naiveté of inexperience had led JFK in 1961 to authorise a poorly planned invasion operation of the Bay of Pigs area in Cuba. This fiasco, which involved Cuban exiles and the CIA, was part of the reason and background for why Castro asked for Soviet military aid (including the missiles) in the first place.
- When the crisis began, the president received conflicting advice about which tactics to adopt. Some of the senior military figures argued for a 'first strike' to destroy the missile sites before they were operational. Others even advocated a major amphibious assault landing on the island. Both bits of advice, if JFK had followed them, could easily have escalated the crisis.

It also highlighted some *strengths* in the presidency:
- By listening to a range of views, President Kennedy was able to make an informed choice and opted for that suggested by his brother Bobby, who was then attorney-general but also a confidant of JFK, of going for a naval blockade of Cuba, having already made secret contact with the Russians. When the crisis ended, JFK said, 'Thank God for Bobby.'
- The president convened a special body called ExCom, where all the options were discussed and the daily situation on the ground monitored. This was a good example of the president deploying effectively his resources and knowledge.

By making the 'right choice' (the USSR backed down, tension was eased and a telephone hotline between Moscow and Washington was set up), JFK saw a surge in his personal ratings. This personal legacy, along with the tragic circumstances of his assassination in 1963, enabled his successor, Lyndon B. Johnson (LBJ) to score a massive election victory in 1964.

Overall, this episode shows that presidents and their choices and decisions can reveal both strengths and weaknesses. It was initial weakness that in part created the crisis, but strength and astute choice that led to a positive outcome. These twin aspects of presidential power are sometimes referred to as '**imperilled**' (weak) and '**imperial**' (strong). It should also be noted that as it was a foreign policy matter, congressional approval was not required, which made matters easier for the president but also left him nowhere to hide and no one else to blame if it all went badly wrong.

Verdict: is the position of US president imperilled or imperial?

There is no simple answer to this question. In essence, perhaps it is easiest to see the presidential position as '**tidal**' — it ebbs and flows according to a number of variables.

The imperilled dimensions of the presidency

- When a hostile Congress blocks their legislative programme.
- When a president encounters an adverse Supreme Court decision.
- When a president makes decisions (usually in secret) and they turn out badly. Even worse, if they try to cover them up — Nixon and Watergate.
- When a two-term president is in his final two years of office (e.g. Obama 2013–2017), the 'lame duck' stage of presidency, and all eyes are on the next likely occupant of the White House.
- When presidential appointments work out badly and there are frequent and turbulent changes. For example Trump's first two press secreteries, sean spicer and Anthony scaramucci, were both gone within six months.

The imperial dimensions of the presidency

- When a supportive Congress is willing to enact their policy measures.
- When a president takes risky decisions, especially in foreign and military affairs, and they prove to be successful.
- When a president is at the start of their term: the 'honeymoon period'.
- When a president makes effective use of the considerable resources available to them, such as the Cabinet and executive bureaucracy.
- The use of executive orders that require no prior approval from Congress, such as those temporarily banning travellers to the States from seven Muslim countires, issued at the start of Trump's presidency.

Who has the greater power: the US president or the UK prime minister?

First, it is important to see the difference in resources available to each of these posts. It also depends on the variables of time and political circumstances. Yet overall the following pointers might prove helpful.

Advantages possessed by the British prime minister

The prime minister as the sole and elected leader of their party can usually rely on the loyalty of their MPs. Backbench revolts are more common now than 30–40 years ago, though, as when attempts to relax further Sunday trading laws were blocked by a backbench rebellion of 27 Tory MPs in 2016.

The prime minister normally commands majority support in the House of Commons (although Cameron's hands were partly tied by being in a coalition government with the Liberal Democrats from 2010 to 2015). The contents of the Queen's Speech are therefore very likely to become law.

Exam tip

When debating imperial/imperilled interpretations of the presidency in an answer, make sure you argue in a balanced fashion. All presidencies have elements of both, and much depends on circumstances.

In essence, strong, popular presidents early in their term of office who choose their advisers carefully and handle tricky situations well can enjoy a lot more power than a lame-duck president confronted with low approval ratings, a sinking economy and a Congress controlled by his opponents. Power is never a fixed entity.

Knowledge check 12

When is a US president at their strongest?

Exam tip

Contrast the Queen's Speech with the president's annual State of the Union address. In the latter, the president often seems to ask Congress to send him legislation on a certain matter; he certainly cannot command it to do so.

The doctrine of cabinet collective responsibility ensures all ministers must support the prime minister and decisions made in cabinet, or else resign.

They are less likely to have their actions (and certainly their legislation) struck down by the UK Supreme Court, though Brexit negotiations and the judicial rulings there in 2016–17 have proved more problematic for Theresa May.

The prime minister can serve for more than two terms, as demonstrated by both Thatcher and Blair.

Advantages possessed by the US president

The president enjoys the huge administrative and policy advice resources of his personal bureaucracy, for example EXOP.

The president has a personal mandate through being directly elected in a separate election; the prime minister is in post only by virtue of being party leader and can be removed by a coup within the party, as happened infamously to Margaret Thatcher in 1990. Congress equally can possess such a mandate and claim to speak 'for the people'. However, do presidents such as Trump, who lose the popular vote, have a right to claim that mandate?

The president has some clearly defined formal constitutional powers. They can veto legislation, a power that is rarely overturned. The powers of patronage enable supporters and trusted aides to be part of the government. There is no need, as in the British cabinet, to appoint voices from across the party spectrum to aid party unity.

The power to appoint Supreme Court justices when vacancies occur can enable a lasting change of judicial tone and direction to occur. In Britain, this opportunity simply does not exist as all judicial appointments are made independently by the Judicial Appointments Commission.

Overall

In terms of formal powers, it could be said that a prime minister with a large Commons majority and a relatively united party has more immediate power, especially in domestic policy. 'Presidential' PMs such as Thatcher and Blair were able to railroad through controversial policies such as the poll tax and tuition fees in a way that US presidents could not. Yet prime ministers with thin majorities and/or a divided party behind them face many challenges. John Major (1990–97), for example, had ongoing problems with his own Eurosceptic MPs after his surprise victory in 1992. Prime ministers in coalition governments are forced from the outset to make compromises and concessions, such as Cameron over cutting inheritance tax and allowing a referendum on the AV (alternative vote) system. Yet American presidents also face challenges from an uncooperative legislature, even one controlled by their own party. President Clinton was unable to pass healthcare reforms in the 1990s despite a Democrat-controlled Congress.

In foreign policy, US presidents are arguably more powerful simply by virtue of the sheer size of America's military muscle. As commander-in-chief of armed forces resourced by the world's biggest military budget, they can wield enormous power and influence beyond their own country. Congress in practice can do little to stop foreign interventions from beginning and despite measures such as the War Powers Act,

Exam tip

When comparing the two positions, make the point that both are often constrained by circumstances such as their party's strength in the legislature and their personal popularity. UK parties can (and have) effectively removed the PM, as Conservative MPs did with Thatcher in 1990. In the US, Congress can prove stubborn in refusing to pass laws desired by the president, especially if there is divided government or the president suffers from low approval ratings.

is usually reluctant to apply the brakes mid-campaign. But military operations that are prolonged, costly and ultimately fail can tarnish a whole presidency. Will history remember LBJ more for Vietnam or for the Great Society programme, or George W. Bush more for an arguably counter-productive war on terror in Iraq and Afghanistan, or his massive anti-Aids programme in Africa?

In reality, both positions have the potential to be positively transformative, but equally to end in failure and disappointment. Circumstances, criteria and character all play their part for both roles. Beware of the simplistic answer.

> **Knowledge check 13**
>
> How could it be argued that most presidencies end in failure?
> ....

Summary

By the end of this section, you should know and understand:

- The main formal powers of the president as found in the Constitution.
- The main informal powers of the president.
- The chief ways that a president's powers can be restricted.
- The other parts of the executive (such as EXOP and the cabinet) and how they relate to the president.
- The debate over presidential power: imperilled or imperial?
- The differences between US presidential and UK prime ministerial powers.

You should also be aware of some of the ways that the presidency impacts on other parts of US government and politics. This is known as the **synoptic** element:

- The formal powers of the president emanate from the Constitution, though the informal ones partly come from the vague wording of some clauses **(The constitutional frameworks of US government)**.
- Its power is often shared with Congress — cooperation between the two can be productive, while conflict or competition can lead to frustration for the president **(The legislative branch of government: Congress)**.
- The Supreme Court can rule actions of the president unconstitutional **(The judicial branch of government: the Supreme Court)**.
- The indirect method of electing the president can sometimes weaken their mandate if they win the Electoral College but lose the popular vote **(The electoral process and direct democracy)**.

The judicial branch of government: the Supreme Court

How are Supreme Court justices appointed?

As noted in the section on presidential powers, Supreme Court justices are appointed by the president, but their appointment needs to be confirmed by a simple majority in the Senate. However, behind that simple statement lies quite a lot of politics and complexity.

The appointment process for the Supreme Court

Interestingly, the Constitution says very little about the makeup and qualifications required for the Supreme Court. There are no requirements regarding nationality, age or even the number of justices. Thus the current number of **nine justices** is set out in a federal law of 1869 and could be varied if Congress and the president agreed. You should also be aware that appointment is for life or until a justice decides to retire, as John Paul Stevens did in 2010 at the age of 90. In theory, a Supreme Court justice may be tried and impeached, but that last happened with Samuel Chase in 1804 and he was acquitted.

Significance

The lack of clarity and precision around the Supreme Court in the Constitution has led to a number of developments. Its most important power, that of **judicial review** (the ability to strike down a law or executive action as unconstitutional), is not specifically mentioned; instead it derives from a legal precedent in the 1803 case *Marbury* v *Madison*. Equally, the lack of a set number of judges has occasionally led presidents to consider 'court-packing', namely filling the Court with additional judges of their own choosing. This was famously considered by FDR when some of his New Deal legislation was struck down by the Court. In the event, his plan failed to garner enough support in the Senate.

When it comes to appointing Supreme Court justices, the following points should be noted:

- Although in theory a president has a free choice, in reality they need to pick someone who is legally well qualified, such as a judge in a lower court or a law professor, and who is likely to be confirmed by the Senate.
- When a president nominates a candidate, they normally first sound out senators from their party to maximise the chances of a smooth passage. It was at this point that George W. Bush was forced to withdraw the nomination of Harriet Miers, as the nomination lacked support from many Republican senators due partly to her perceived inexperience.
- Once formally nominated, the candidate is questioned by the Senate Judiciary Committee, allowing senators to find out where nominees stand on key issues such as abortion and gun rights. The vote is only advisory but a poor performance or a close vote in committee can suggest a difficult time when the nomination goes before the whole Senate. For example, Clarence Thomas endured a difficult committee hearing in 1991 partly due to allegations of sexual harassment. Having squeaked through, he was confirmed by the slim margin of 52–48.

- It is rare for the Senate to reject a nomination. The last time this happened was in 1987 when Reagan appointee William Bork was rejected by a margin of 58–42. Bork was largely rejected for ideological reasons, being seen as too conservative. The Senate can frustrate a president's appointments in other ways, however. When Obama nominated Merrick Garland for a vacancy in March 2016 following the death of Antonin Scalia, the Republican Senate majority simply refused to begin nomination hearings, arguing it was too soon before a presidential election. It was a gamble that paid off, leaving President Trump free to nominate his own candidate, Neil Gorsuch.
- Presidents are keen to get a justice appointed who reflects their own political and ideological outlook, not only because such appointments are very likely to outlast their own tenure in office (the **'echo chamber'** effect) but also because of the key role the Court plays in policy, politics and rights. This is explored in more detail later on.

Note, however, that not all presidents have the opportunity to make appointments to the Supreme Court. It all depends on the retirement or demise of serving justices. Carter (1977–81), for example, made none, while George W. Bush and Obama both made two appointments.

Significance

The appointment process is highly politicised and is about much more than ensuring a potential judge is legally experienced and qualified enough for the post. It should be seen as another arena for potential political clashes and conflict between the executive and the legislature, above all in times of divided government.

Knowledge check 14

On what basis are Supreme Court justices chosen?

The composition of the Supreme Court

Commentators often ascribe the labels 'liberal' or 'conservative' to the Supreme Court justices. These do not equate to formal party allegiance, however, but along with terms such as **loose/strict constructionist, judicial activist/restraint** are useful shorthand by which to classify roughly the justices. At the time of writing, the Court was **finely balanced** between the two groups. Many key decisions during the Obama years, such as those on gun control, gay marriage and campaign finance, were narrow 5–4 verdicts. The most 'centrist' judge, Anthony Kennedy, frequently decided the final outcome. The current justices (in 2017) who could be considered as liberal/loose constructionist/proponents of judicial activism are:

- Stephen Breyer
- Ruth Bader Ginsburg
- Sonia Sotomayor
- Elena Kagan

Those who could be considered as conservative/strict constructionist/proponents of judicial restraint are:

- John Roberts (Chief Justice)
- Clarence Thomas
- Samuel Alito

As mentioned above, Anthony Kennedy is viewed as being in the middle: conservative in some of his rulings but more progressive in others. Justices in the middle are often known as the **'swing' justices**.

Significance

The finely balanced composition of the Court means not only that verdicts can be unpredictable but also that appointments are often said to 'tilt' the Court. The 12-year Republican occupancy of the White House from 1981–93 certainly enabled a more rightward shift in the Court in favour of a less activist approach. This was continued during the eight years that Bush Jr was president, but even so, no president can assume the Court will find consistently in their favour. The judiciary remains independent and not directly accountable to anyone, including their appointing president. Justices can often 'disappoint' their patron — for example, President Eisenhower is reputed to have said in 1958, 'I have made two mistakes, and they are both sitting on the Supreme Court', referring to his appointment of the activist justices Brennan and Warren.

Exam tip

Always exercise caution when labelling Supreme Court justices. Do not refer to them as Republicans or Democrats but use phrases such as 'generally regarded as liberal/conservative, or loose/strict constructionist'.

The importance of the Supreme Court in politics and government

As implied already, the importance of the Supreme Court in key areas of American society and politics cannot be underestimated. Due to the principle of **constitutional sovereignty**, all laws and executive actions must fall within the bounds of the Constitution, and through its 'discovered power' of **judicial review** the Constitution is in practice what the Supreme Court of the day says it is. The only way round a Supreme Court ruling is to pass a constitutional amendment or wait for a change in the composition of the Court. The first is cumbersome and unlikely to succeed, while the second depends a great deal on luck and patience. For example, it took the Court well over 50 years to change its mind over the constitutionality of racial segregation.

In reality, nearly every controversial measure passed by US law-makers will end up before the Supreme Court. Among these issues have been:

- race
- abortion
- gun rights
- death penalty
- political campaign finance laws
- prayers in state schools
- Guantanamo Bay
- Obamacare
- result of the 2000 election

Many would say that the Court has a unique role in both reflecting and shaping popular attitudes. For example, the rulings against racial segregation in the Deep South and upholding civil rights legislation forced otherwise unwilling states to act and end racial discrimination, at least officially. While race remains a sensitive issue in much of America, the Court has certainly played a key part in ending the more overt examples of such discrimination. There are times though when the Court does

Knowledge check 15

Define the term 'judicial review'.

not reflect accurately the broader views, for instance when it effectively struck down parts of the 2002 Bipartisan Campaign Reform Act (BCRA) measure that sought to limit spending in political campaigns by its 2010 decision in the *Citizens United* case. Polls showed well over three-quarters of Americans disagreed with the verdict, which was also criticised by President Obama, but all to no avail. Yes, the Supreme Court matters very much because the Constitution matters.

Divisions within the Supreme Court: how are Supreme Court justices often labelled?

Traditionally, two main labels have been coined to describe the interpretations of the Constitution by Supreme Court justices: **judicial activism** and **judicial restraint**.

Judicial activism

Also known as **loose constructionism**, this approach favours a flexible and more innovative reading of the Constitution. In essence, the approach sees the Constitution as a living and evolving document that needs to be understood and interpreted in the light of contemporary society. A good example is the modern-day notion of a right to personal privacy. Nowhere is this stated explicitly in the Constitution, but there are hints of it in some clauses of the Bill of Rights, for example freedom of belief (First Amendment) and the Fifth Amendment's focus on the right not to incriminate oneself. Finally, the Ninth Amendment states that the 'enumeration of certain rights' in the Bill of Rights 'shall not be construed to deny or disparage other rights retained by the people'. The exact meaning of the Ninth Amendment is somewhat imprecise, but some (judicial activists/loose constructionists) have interpreted the Ninth Amendment as justification for broadly reading the Bill of Rights and hence the Constitution as protecting personal privacy.

Significance

Why does this matter? In essence because it has allowed those Supreme Courts dominated by activist justices such as Warren Court (1954–69) to 'discover' new rights/freedoms based on privacy rights, such as the right of married couples to purchase contraceptives as exemplified by the 1965 case of *Griswold* v *Connecticut*. It has also been instrumental in protecting women's rights to an abortion in the famous *Roe* v *Wade* case of 1973. Judicial activism has usually been associated with liberal and progressive forces in US society, linked as it has been traditionally with causes such as feminism, anti-racism and gay rights.

Judicial restraint

This approach is traditionally seen as the polar opposite of judicial activism and favours instead a more literalist and narrow interpretation of the Constitution — **strict constructionism**. In short, its advocates are more inclined to view the Constitution as only protecting those rights explicitly identified in the document. Therefore, while they would have no problem in striking down a state law that for argument's sake made potential voters pay to register to vote (a direct contravention of the Twenty-fourth Amendment), they would be less inclined to overturn a law that, say, banned the smoking of tobacco, as the right to smoke is not specified in the Constitution.

Significance

This approach prefers to grant more power to federal and state legislatures to pass laws as they see fit, not least because they are popularly elected and democratically accountable. The judicial restraint approach was summed up well by Chief Justice Roberts, who in 2006 said, 'If it is not necessary to decide more … then in my view, it is necessary not to decide more.' Usually this approach has found favour with Republican presidents from Nixon onwards, who have normally pledged only to appoint such justices to the bench. The reality is more nuanced, however.

> **Knowledge check 16**
>
> Why do conservatives/ Republicans tend to prefer strict constructionist Supreme Court justices?

Problems of definition

In reality, most justices eschew both the definitions above, especially the latter. Even the late Justice Scalia (the judge most associated with strict constructionism) commented: 'I am not a strict constructionist, and no one ought to be.' He preferred to see himself taking a 'reasonable' understanding of the text of the Constitution, not a rigidly literal one. In practice, the distinction between the two groups/terms is perhaps best seen as that between liberals and conservatives. What Republicans generally want from their judicial appointees are judges who are pro-life (anti-abortion), pro-religion, pro-big business, tough on law and order and pro-guns. What Democrats favour are judges who are pretty much the opposite: pro-choice, pro the separation of religion and public life, pro-gun control and keenly aware of the need to protect and enhance minority rights.

Finally, it should be noted:

- Supreme Court justices are not always predictable in the siding over verdicts — for example, it was the 'conservative' Chief Justice John Roberts who delivered the casting vote for the 5–4 verdict in the 2012 *Sibelius* case that upheld Obamacare.
- 'Conservative' justices can also find new rights, such as the right to personal ownership of guns as in the 2008 *DC v Heller* case.
- A large number of the 70–80 cases heard by the Court each year are decided unanimously/nearly unanimously. For example, 44% of the cases heard in 2015–16 were unanimous, as indeed was a December 2016 ruling on a dispute between Apple and Samsung over alleged patent infringements.

What are some of the landmark rulings of the Supreme Court?

The AQA specification requires knowledge of **any two** landmark rulings. There is a wide range to choose from, including the two summarised below. You will find further relevant examples in the later section on civil rights.

Miranda v *Arizona* (1966)

In *Miranda* v *Arizona* (1966), the Supreme Court ruled that detained criminal suspects, prior to police questioning, must be informed of their constitutional right to an attorney and against self-incrimination. The case began with the 1963 arrest of Phoenix resident Ernesto Miranda, who was charged with rape, kidnapping and robbery. Miranda was not informed of his rights prior to the police interrogation. During the interrogation, Miranda allegedly confessed to committing the crimes, which the police apparently recorded. At trial, the prosecution's case consisted solely of his confession while Miranda had no lawyer present. Miranda was convicted of both rape and kidnapping. He appealed to the Arizona Supreme Court, claiming that the police had unconstitutionally obtained his confession. The court disagreed, however, and upheld the conviction.

Miranda appealed to the US Supreme Court, which reviewed the case in 1966. The Supreme Court, in a 5–4 decision, ruled that the prosecution could not use Miranda's confession as evidence because the police had failed to first inform Miranda of his constitutional rights (Fifth and Sixth Amendments) to legal representation and against self-incrimination, i.e. his right to remain silent.

Significance

- This case forced police authorities formally to remind any suspects of their rights under the Constitution, often known as 'Miranda rights'. In short, it changed policing practice nationwide.
- The case is often seen as an example of *judicial activism in practice*, by extending some rights to criminal suspects. The relevant amendments in the Bill of Rights make no specific reference to suspects' rights in this exact context, but the activist Warren Court decided they did implicitly.
- The case led to a *conservative backlash* based in part on the view of a dissenting (pro-judicial restraint) justice Byron White. He argued at the time that the majority verdict had 'no significant support in the history of the privilege or in the language of the Fifth Amendment'. Several subsequent cases have sought (largely unsuccessfully) to overturn the verdict. Some have argued that the 2010 case *Berghuis* v *Thompkins* did partially undermine 'Miranda rights'.

Bush v *Gore* (2000)

This result was one of the most sensitive and political that any Supreme Court has had to make. Essentially it decided the outcome of the 2000 presidential election in a finely balanced 5–4 decision. Although Gore had won the majority of the popular vote, whoever won Florida would win the Electoral College and thus the presidency. The result in Florida was itself very close and a lot hinged on the infamous 'butterfly ballots', where the manually punched holes on some ballots were not properly perforated. The Court ultimately ruled that Florida's court-ordered manual recount of vote ballots was unconstitutional.

Because the results were so close, Florida law called for an automatic machine recount of ballots. The recount resulted in a dramatic tightening of the race, leaving Bush with a bare 327-vote lead out of almost 6 million ballots cast. With the race so close, Florida law allowed Gore the option of manual vote recounts in counties of his choosing. Gore opted for manual recounts in four counties with widespread complaints of voting machine malfunction — the butterfly ballots. However, Florida law also required that the state's election results be certified by the (Republican) Secretary of State, Katherine Harris, within seven days of the election. Three of the four counties were unable to complete the process even by the extended deadline of 26 November. Harris then wanted to end an incomplete recount with Bush still ahead, the Florida Supreme Court refused, and so Bush appealed to the Supreme Court which sided with him and Harris.

Significance

- Above all, this showed how the Court can get dragged into party politics. Whatever decision it made would have angered roughly half of Americans. Surely there is no greater political power in the USA than having the final say over who will lead the nation for the next four years?
- With all five of the majority justices being Republican appointees, many saw this as an extension of party politics into the supposedly independent judicial part of government.
- The Court did not actively choose to decide/intervene in the election result but was responding to a case that came before it.
- The Court reached its verdict using legal argument, not the personal political views of its members. It rejected the Florida Supreme Court's recount order because it granted more protection to some ballots than to others, violating the Fourteenth Amendment's Equal Protection Clause. This clause forbids states from denying 'to any person within their jurisdiction the equal protection of the laws'. The Court (well, five out of nine justices at any rate) argued that voting for a president constituted such a fundamental right and that the Florida Supreme Court's order violated this right because it was 'arbitrary'. Equally, the arguments advanced by the minority side were couched in legal not political terms.
- Unlike many landmark cases, this one did not directly establish new rights or precedents, but arguably by delivering the White House to Bush Jr, it did change the course of American history.

Knowledge check 17

What is meant by the term 'landmark judgement'?

How the US and UK Supreme Courts compare

As with much else that is comparative in US and UK politics, the gap once seen as wide and distinct has narrowed of late, although arguably this is the area where one of the biggest differences remains.

Key differences

The notion of **constitutional sovereignty** as opposed to **parliamentary sovereignty** means that the US Supreme Court has far more of a direct impact on the laws and lives of its ordinary citizens. Nearly every controversial and divisive issue in US politics is likely to end up before the Court. Whatever it decides in such cases will be highly unpopular with some. It is very much a regular part of the political arena. The UK Supreme Court, by contrast, is much less likely to be called upon to decide the legality of Parliament's or the executive's actions.

The US Supreme Court has played a key role in the development and protection of civil liberties and its landmark cases are regarded as milestones in US history. This is untrue for the UK where acts of Parliament are far more prominent. Thus gay marriage in the UK was legalised in 2013 not by a court decision as in America but by parliamentary legislation.

The selection and appointment of US Supreme Court justices is highly politicised and high profile while that in the UK is not. Nor is there the same use of political labels for UK justices.

The UK Supreme Court is not the sole or entirely ultimate highest legal authority in the country. The highest court in Scotland is the High Court of Justiciary, which has legal supremacy in delegated matters, while the European Court of Justice in Brussels has the ultimate say over areas of law covered by EU law, at least while the UK remains an EU member. The Strasbourg-based European Court of Human Rights, to which Britain is a signatory, is the ultimate arbiter of whether UK laws and executive actions contravene the European Convention on Human Rights.

Some similarities

The UK Supreme Court, thanks in part to the passage of the 1998 Human Rights Act, has had an increasing role in adjudicating over issues many would regard as the rightful preserve of Parliament, such as votes for prisoners and the deportation of terrorist suspects. In 2016/17 it dealt with challenges to the Brexit vote and required Prime Minister May to seek Commons approval to begin the formal process of triggering Article 50. Undoubtedly it has become the focus of greater publicity and controversy in recent years. This has been the case in the USA also.

Both courts are independent in the sense that they are politically and democratically unaccountable and their members do not form part of the executive or judiciary. Both sets of judges are appointed on a permanent basis (for life in the USA and to age 75 in the UK) and cannot be easily removed by the executive or legislature.

Neither body can initiate cases but instead must wait for them to come before them for judgement. In that sense, both courts are essentially reactive.

Summary

By the end of this section, you should know and understand:

■ Why the Supreme Court is so important when studying US politics.
■ The main formal powers and functions of the Supreme Court, especially that of judicial review.
■ How its members are appointed and the associated politicisation of the nomination and confirmation system.
■ The current composition of the Court.
■ The two main types of judicial approaches to the Constitution: activist and restraint.
■ The importance and key points of two landmark cases.
■ The ways in which the US and UK Supreme Courts differ, but also some of their similarities.

You should also be aware of some of the ways that the Supreme Court impacts on other parts of US government and politics. This is known as the **synoptic** element.

■ The Court has historically played a key role in interpreting and defining civil rights and liberties **(Civil rights)**.
■ The Court can and has struck down as unconstitutional laws of Congress and presidential/executive actions **(The legislative and executive branches of government: Congress and president)**.
■ The Court is the ultimate arbiter of what the Constitution says **(The constitutional frameworks of US government)**.
■ Judicial appointments to the court are highly politicised and usually based on partisan political outlook as much as on legal expertise and competence **(Political parties)**.

■ The electoral process and direct democracy

How does America elect its president and Congress?

Elections in the USA — presidential and congressional

All US national elections are based on the **majoritarian** or first-past-the-post electoral system. There is no use of any other voting system as there is in the UK for the devolved assemblies, which use the additional member system.

National elections occur every two years in November when the whole of the House of Representatives and one-third of the Senate are elected. Every four years sees a presidential election; the congressional elections that occur when there is no presidential election are coined **mid-terms**. Elections for Congress are direct, while that for the president is indirect as it uses an Electoral College system.

How are candidates selected in America?

For all major elections, **candidate selection** is undertaken by **popular vote** rather than (as in the UK) by the selection committees of local parties. The most common form is the **primary**, while some states such as Iowa use caucuses for presidential candidate selection.

> **Knowledge check 18**
>
> Who are elected at the mid-terms?

For presidential elections whichever method, primaries or caucuses, is used, the purpose is identical: to select delegates for the **national nominating convention** of each party which in turn chooses the candidate to go forward to the November election. As primaries and caucuses last over several months, normally from February to June of the election year, the final result is usually a foregone conclusion by the time of the party convention in July/August. Some of the key points about primaries and caucuses to note are:

■ They are **state organised and run**, so the timing and other aspects of the elections vary considerably from state to state. For example, some states such as Texas hold **open primaries** where registered voters can decide on the day which party's primary they wish to vote in. Others such as New York hold **closed primaries** where only registered supporters of each party may participate. A few such as California hold **top-two primaries** for congressional elections, where the two candidates with the largest number of votes go forward to the general election irrespective of party affiliation. This meant, for example, that in November 2016 the California Senate contest was between two Democrats. In essence, the primary system is complex and varies considerably from state to state.

■ While primaries involve a secret ballot and a formal vote, **caucuses** are significantly different. They are best described as **several layers of informal and open meetings of local party supporters**. Each layer selects delegates pledged to the different candidates to go forward to the next round or caucus. The layers are usually precinct, county and state. This means that there is often quite a time lapse between the first (precinct) level caucus and the final selection of state delegates for each candidate. **Caucuses are most common in smaller and more sparsely populated states such as Kansas and Alaska**. Thirteen states held presidential caucuses in 2016.

Significance

The relatively democratic system of primaries and caucuses weakens the ability of the national parties to influence the final choice of candidates in both congressional and presidential contests. However, the addition of another layer of voting, and especially the complicated and lengthy nature of caucuses, has led to debate about the relative merits of the system.

Knowledge check 19

In what ways does the primaries/caucuses system reflect the federal nature of the USA?

The debate over primaries and caucuses

Supporters would argue that primaries/caucuses increase opportunities for democratic participation in politics. Opponents would counter that voter turnout is pretty low, usually well below 30%, especially for caucuses. In 2016, with two high-profile candidates on both sides and competitive open races in both parties, the Iowa caucuses achieved a combined turnout of less than 16%.

Detractors of primaries/caucuses argue that it weakens political parties and encourages candidate-centred campaigns. Its advocates would argue that it improves upon the old and corrupted system of 'smoke-filled rooms' that prevailed until the 1960s, where a small clique of party bosses chose the candidate.

Its supporters would also argue that it enables potential nominees to be 'road tested' prior to the actual election in areas such as debating skills, stamina, fundraising ability and developing clear policy positions, and allows any embarrassing background issues to surface before the 'real' campaign. Opponents would highlight the additional expense, the focus on personality over policy and the need to re-set policy positions after the primaries season in order to attract a less partisan group of voters than caucus/primary voters. In addition, the revelations of the 'Billy Bush sex tape' that damaged Trump just weeks before the November poll in 2016 suggest that primaries may not be entirely effective at exposing all the controversial issues concerning candidates.

Finally, one attraction of primaries/caucuses is that they allow outsider/relatively unknown candidates such as Obama in 2008 and Carter in 1976 to emerge, build momentum and ultimately win the nomination. No other system, arguably, would have allowed a political outsider such as Donald Trump (a registered Democrat from 2001–09) to secure the Republican nomination in 2016. The choice proved prescient as Trump went on to win the election. Detractors would argue that such a system can either lead to inexperienced presidents such as Carter, who struggled in office, or play into the hands of well-funded populists who might prove equally problematic in office.

National nominating conventions

In many ways the function of national nominating conventions nowadays is purely ceremonial as the delegate tally from primaries and caucuses usually pre-determines the choice of candidate by the time of the national convention. Some have therefore spoken of the conventions as akin to **coronations** and rallies. They still perform an important function in US presidential elections, however, marking the formal start of the general election campaign, when the successful candidates turn their attack on the candidate from the opposing party as well as outlining their own policy platforms.

They can also enable internal wounds and divisions of a bruising primary campaign to be healed, as for example in 2016 when Bernie Sanders urged his Democrat supporters to rally behind Clinton. Ted Cruz at the Republican convention signally failed to endorse Trump explicitly. Handled well with strong speeches and a display of unity, the conventions normally provide a short-term poll boost for the successful candidate. Recently, the parties have taken to holding their conventions in swing states: the Republican convention in 2016 was in Cleveland, Ohio, while that for the Democrats was in Philadelphia, Pennsylvania.

If the primaries have not produced a clear winner, then the convention will be where the nomination is decided. This eventuality is known as a **brokered convention**. There was much speculation about this with the Republicans in 2016 but it failed to materialise.

The Electoral College system

Another distinguishing feature of the US political system, especially when compared with that of the UK, is how the president is elected. The Founding Fathers favoured a system of **indirect election**, which gave rise to the Electoral College. The college comprises 538 electors which represents the strength of each state's congressional delegation, i.e. the number of senators (always two) plus the number of House

Knowledge check 20

When could a national nominating convention have real political significance?

representatives (a minimum of one). Thus the smallest states, such as the Dakotas that have just 1 congressman and 2 senators, have 3 Electoral College votes (ECV) while California, with 53 congressmen and two senators, has 55 ECV. In addition, Washington DC, despite having no voting members of Congress, is allowed 3 ECV. The presidency goes to whoever manages to secure a simple majority of the 538 ECV, namely 270. In the event of a tie or no candidate winning 270 ECV, the choice goes to the House of Representatives who have one vote per state. If the House still cannot pick a president (e.g. there is a tie 25/25), then the vice president who would be chosen by the Senate in the event of an inconclusive Electoral College result would become president. In reality, the Electoral College has delivered a clear winner without problems in every election since 1876.

The electors themselves are chosen by the state parties and are usually given to loyal party stalwarts as an honour. In all states bar Maine and Nebraska, the candidate with the largest number of votes wins all the ECV for that state regardless of the margin of victory.

Significance

The somewhat convoluted nature of choosing the president has given rise to some debate concerning the merits or otherwise of the current system. There are points on both sides which you need to be aware of and understand. Also be aware that electors remain free to change their mind, which could be seen as undermining the democratic process — see the point below regarding 'faithless electors'.

The Electoral College — advantages

- It reflects the federal nature of the USA and means that campaigning is state focused and that smaller and medium-sized states regarded as 'swing states', such as New Hampshire and North Carolina, remain targeted and relevant to the national campaign.
- It contributes to the cohesiveness of the country by requiring a distribution of popular support to be elected president. A president cannot be popular in just one densely populated part of the nation.
- It enhances the status of minority interests. This is because the votes of small minorities in a state may make the difference between winning all of that state's electoral votes or none. Also, as ethnic minority groups often happen to concentrate in states such as California and Florida with many electoral votes or which are key swing states, they assume an importance to presidential candidates well out of proportion to their number. The same principle applies to other special interest groups such as labour unions and farmers who might otherwise be overlooked in one big national poll.
- It usually delivers the 'right result', namely the winner of the nationwide popular vote also wins the Electoral College, as happened in 2008 and 2012. The results in 2000 and 2016 were the exception, not the rule. The previous time the 'wrong result was delivered was in 1888.

Exam tip

Do not describe the Maine/Nebraska system as proportional — it is not. Instead it can allow the party that loses the overall vote in the state to potentially pick up an ECV if it wins the most votes in one electoral district. Hence, while the Republicans lost overall in Maine in 2016, they did win the most votes in one House district so ended up with one ECV to the Democrats' three. It is a more refined version of FPTP.

The Electoral College — disadvantages

- Above all, as in 2000 and again in 2016, it can deliver the 'wrong result', namely the victor of the popular vote fails to win the Electoral College. Thus Hillary Clinton won nearly 3 million more votes compared with Donald Trump in 2016 but lost the Electoral College convincingly by 232 to 306. This results in a minority president being chosen.
- Electors can and do 'break their pledge' and vote for another candidate. They are known as **faithless electors**. A record number of seven electors rebelled in 2016, primarily to make a protest about the unfairness of the system. It should be noted, though, that faithless electors have never affected the overall outcome.
- Votes in less populated states count for more than those in the most populated. For example, while least populated Wyoming has roughly 143,000 people per each ECV, New York and Florida both have around 500,000 people per each ECV. In summary, voter power is greater in smaller states than in larger states.
- The Electoral College system encourages candidates to focus their campaigns almost exclusively on 'must-win' swing states such as Ohio. Larger but 'safe' states such as New York and Texas largely get overlooked.
- The system depresses turnout. As the majority of states are not really that competitive in most elections, there is little incentive for voters of the party likely to lose to turn out and vote: the 'wasted vote' syndrome. Arguably, though, if the allocation of electors was done proportionally by states (something that would not require a constitutional amendment), this problem could be solved.

> **Knowledge check 21**
>
> Why do you think neither of the two main parties is keen to change the 'winner takes all' nature of most states in selecting electors to the Electoral College?

What affects the outcome of elections in the USA?

The factors that help determine electoral outcomes

It is vital to remember the role played by the following in US elections:

- **Money**: how much is raised and spent in campaigns.
- **Media**: the importance of the televised debates, and also their role in shaping and informing the campaign.
- **Issues:** how candidates and parties stand on policies is of great importance. The economy remains paramount, but issues such as immigration, foreign wars and national security can also be significant.
- **Leadership:** this refers to the qualities of statesmanship a presidential candidate exudes. How do they perform under pressure or in a tight corner?
- **Incumbency:** politicians seeking re-election both to Congress and the White House have considerable advantages over challengers.

Money

Money is an important feature in US election campaigns, with billions of dollars being spent on and by candidates at every election. Fundraising, often known as building a 'war chest', is considered vital to most successful campaigns. In contrast to the UK, there are no overall limits on how much candidates can spend, although, as we will see later, there are some limits on how much individuals can give directly to political parties and candidates. Money goes on, among other things, literature, hiring professional consultants and campaign managers and maintaining a presence on social media. The biggest item, however, remains the TV ad, both promoting the candidate and, more often than not, attacking their opponents — the attack ad.

Money does not guarantee success, of course — Clinton out-fundraised Trump by a margin of nearly two to one in 2016 — she raised $1.191 billion while he raised $647 million. Indeed, Trump won the presidency despite raising less than any major party presidential nominee since John McCain in 2008, who was the last to accept federal funds to pay for his general election contest. Also be aware that competitive congressional races, such as those in New Hampshire and Pennsylvania in 2016, can cost well in excess of $100 million, which is more than the entire expenditure by all candidates in the 2015 British general election. In summary, money by no means guarantees victory (though Obama did outspend both his rivals in 2008 and 2012), but it can help, and fundraising cannot be neglected by serious candidates for major political office in America.

Media

Televised debates are a longstanding tradition in US presidential races and are highly anticipated. The first one was in 1960 between Kennedy and Nixon, and Kennedy's stronger performance arguably helped him to a narrow victory. There are normally three presidential debates plus one between the vice presidential candidates. They are seen as an opportunity for candidates to appear confident in their grasp of policy detail, to be effective responders under pressure and also to establish a level of perceived competence and charisma.

Most candidates are well prepared, for example taking part in mock debates with their campaign team beforehand, so major gaffes are rare. Yet their importance can be exaggerated — Trump was generally agreed to have been the weaker conventional performer in 2016, often displaying a weak grasp of policy details, for example. But in a year when many Americans were in an anti-establishment mood, a polished, smooth but perhaps unengaging performer could win the debate battle but lose the presidential war. A serious gaffe, though, can cause a campaign to collapse. In a 2008 televised Republican primary debate, Rick Perry failed to remember the third government agency he would abolish. His 'Oops' moment effectively ended his presidential ambitions. Given the agency concerned was that of Energy, his selection by President Trump as Energy Secretary could be seen as somewhat ironic.

> **Knowledge check 22**
>
> Why in practice do presidential TV debates rarely affect the outcome of the election?

Issues

There is a danger when analysing reasons for electoral success that one focuses too much on personalities and money. Issues, especially the economy, remain very important in influencing how independent voters will cast their support and also whether core supporters will turn out. Candidates usually aim to highlight issues they feel strongly about, while also focusing on perceived weaknesses of their opponents. Thus, in 2016, Trump wanted to focus on issues such as immigration, bringing more jobs and manufacturing back to the USA and dealing with Islamist terrorism in a direct and robust manner, including mooting the idea of temporarily banning many Muslims from entering the USA. He portrayed his opponent as part of the political establishment with close ties to Wall Street. Clinton countered by emphasising a more nuanced approach, largely continuing the policies of fellow Democrat President Obama and firmly backing a liberal approach on social issues such as abortion. She portrayed her opponent as politically inexperienced and dangerously populist, with his character and especially allegations of misogyny as issues in themselves.

Every election throws up different issues: foreign policy and national security, for example, were key topics in the 1980s and in 2004, the former due to the Cold War and the latter due to 9/11. The issues were in many ways **valence ones** and not about polar opposites — which candidate would best stand up to the Soviet Union or was best equipped to take on Al Qaeda? Reagan's promise to escalate defence spending and to create an ambitious (and ultimately unsuccessful) missile shield known as 'Star Wars' struck a chord with many who wanted a stronger, no-nonsense USA. Therefore, issues matter, but they need to be communicated effectively and convincingly, which ties in with money and the media.

Leadership

Especially in presidential elections, candidates need to come across as commanding respect, conveying empathy and vision in equal measure, and having the dignity and personal integrity deemed necessary for the top prize in American politics. In short, they need to come across as presidential. Calmness in a crisis and honesty are key virtues: both Nixon and Clinton were observed to have damaged the office of president by lying publicly about Watergate in one instance and their extra-marital activities (the Lewinsky affair) in the other. By contrast, George W. Bush's assured and appropriate demeanour in the aftermath of 9/11 sent his approval ratings soaring. Trump's temper and apparent tendency to harbour grudges were criticised by many in the 2016 campaign and led some even within his own party to regard him as 'unfit' to be president. Such fears did not cost him the election however.

Incumbency

Among all the factors related to electoral success, especially at congressional level, incumbency is one of the most important. As mentioned in the section on Congress, re-election is the norm for most senators and congressmen, as indeed is the case in the UK where only a minority of constituencies are regarded as marginal. Re-election results are normally in excess of 90%, and the majority of post-war presidents have been re-elected and on an increased share of the vote — Obama in 2012 being the only incumbent president re-elected but on a lower share of the vote.

Why do incumbents do so well?
- They have greater name recognition and usually a higher media profile.
- They already have an established campaign and fundraising organisation.
- They can boast of past achievements, such as federal funds and projects secured for their home state/district.
- House members often benefit from gerrymandering, provided their own party controlled redistricting at the last count. Arguably, hostile redistricting can often pose the greatest threat to an incumbent congressman such as Larry Kissell (NC), who lost his district in 2012 after a hostile gerrymander.

The debate over campaign finance

Campaign finance is one of the most problematic aspects in American politics, primarily because of the ever-growing cost of election campaigns, the potential for corruption with major donors and powerful pressure groups, and the failure of attempts to reform the system, such as the 2002 Bipartisan Campaign Reform Act. The main attempts to try to reform campaign finance have focused on:

- encouraging candidates to voluntarily limit their expenditure by offering matching funding from federal funds to those who accept such a cap
- trying to limit donations to candidates and political parties by individuals and corporate bodies and pressure groups
- requiring transparency with political donations so that the sources of political funding are fully in the public domain
- establishing the Federal Electoral Commission to oversee the rules regarding campaign finance

In reality, though, none of these measures have had the desired effect. Each election has proved more expensive than the last. Some of the reasons behind this are:

The First Amendment guarantees freedom of speech and, by extension, political expression. Any attempts to restrict political expenditure (a form of political expression arguably) are bound to be challenged in the courts. Also the current Supreme Court has proved unhelpful to the cause of campaign finance. While the BCRA itself was judged constitutional (*McConnell* v *FEC 2003*), subsequent court cases such as *Citizens United* in 2010 and *McCutcheon* v *FEC* in 2014 have chipped away at it. These latter two cases have respectively allowed the emergence of Super PACs and ended the overall cap on donations to individual candidates by one donor while retaining the maximum permissible amount of $5,000 directly to the individual candidate by the donor.

Politicians and donors/pressure groups have continued to find loopholes in the legislation. For example, while direct donations are capped, independent expenditure (i.e. that which promotes a certain candidate or attacks their opponents but does not directly coordinate) is not. The use of 527 and 501(c) groups has also enabled campaign finance rules to be circumvented. While such groups cannot directly support or attack individual candidates, they can air 'issue ads' which normally reflect negatively on one candidate. Swift Boat Veterans for Truth was a 527 group that attacked Democrat candidate John Kerry's Vietnam war service record. As a couple of Supreme Court justices ruefully noted with regard to election spending, 'Money, like water, will always find a way through.'

Put simply, there are considerable numbers of very wealthy individuals, such as the Koch Brothers and Sheldon Adelson, along with well-funded pressure groups, that are only too ready to donate to political campaigns in order to further their views and interests. Meanwhile, candidates fear being outspent by rivals so are normally only too willing to receive such help.

Exam tip

Make sure you understand the difference between a PAC and a Super PAC. A PAC can raise and donate money to candidates' own campaigns and to political parties. However, the amount is capped at $5,000 per candidate at each election and $15,000 annually to a political party. Super PACs, by contrast, can spend unlimited amounts, but must not donate directly to candidates or parties. This type of expenditure is often termed independent expenditure.

Significance

The impasse over campaign finance is often cited as one of the worst current failings of American politics. Most ordinary voters want tighter controls and are cynical about the motives of most donors. Most politicians would prefer to be less focused on constant fundraising. Yet given the nature of the Constitution and its interpretation by the current Supreme Court, reform has so far proved elusive. This has probably increased general public disillusionment with politics, as well as dissuading some from seeking higher-level political office. The limits on individual donations to political parties have also weakened them in relation to candidates. In a system where candidates generally have to raise most funds themselves, parties have a reduced role.

> **Knowledge check 23**
>
> Is the Supreme Court or the First Amendment more to blame for the failure of campaign finance reform?

How does direct democracy work in the USA?

Direct democracy takes three main forms in the USA:

■ **Referendums**, where often a group of citizens but sometimes the state legislature seeks either to veto an existing measure or to submit one passed by the state government to voters for approval or rejection. For example, in 2016 Nebraska saw a referendum to veto the recent abolition of the death penalty by its state government.

■ **Ballot initiatives or propositions**, where laws or measures are drawn up 'by the people' and put on the ballot for approval or rejection. Among the issues that have been voted on in this way are state minimum wages, marijuana use, same-sex marriage and assisted dying.

■ **Recall elections**, where state-level officials such as governors, mayors or members of the state legislature have to face a re-election before their normal term of office expires. The most recent high-profile example was that of Scott Walker, governor of Wisconsin, who was recalled in 2012 having been originally elected in 2010 for four years. He won the recall election by an increased margin.

There are also a few other formats such as advisory questions and bond issues that can be put before voters in some states.

There are a few general points to note about the use of direct democracy in the USA. It **functions only at state level**. There is no provision for a nationwide or region-wide referendum as can happen in the UK (consider the vote on Scottish independence (2014) or continued membership of the EU (2016)). The president and members of Congress cannot be recalled mid-term. Also, all outcomes from direct democracy must comply with the Constitution, and can be challenged in the Supreme Court. Thus, while many states passed local measures prohibiting same-sex marriage, these laws were all rendered null and void by the 2015 Supreme Court decision in *Obergefell* v *Hodges*. Finally, the provision for direct democracy varies hugely from state to state. As with primaries and caucuses, complexity and variety prevail over uniformity and simplicity. The best-known ballot initiatives are probably those in California, but in 2016 35 states had some kind of direct democracy on their ballots and 162 measures in total were put before voters. There is much debate over their use, as summarised below.

> **Knowledge check 24**
>
> Do the outcomes of direct democracy ballots such as propositions have more power than ordinary state laws?

The debate over direct democracy: points in favour

- It places decision making closer to the people, it is a 'purer form' of democracy.
- It can enhance voter turnout, especially when controversial measures are on the ballot.
- It enables reforms to pass that local politicians might be unwilling to deal with, such as **term limits** for elected offices.
- Recall elections increase the accountability of elected state officials and keep them more responsive between elections.
- Initiatives can increase political participation, especially as ballot measures are often associated with certain pressure groups such as labour unions and issues such as raising the minimum wage.

The debate over direct democracy: problematic aspects

- Most ballot initiatives are not the work of 'ordinary citizens' but of powerful and well-resourced interest groups or wealthy individuals. Getting measures on to a ballot takes a lot of time and money.
- They can lower voter turnout by increasing the length and complexity of the ballot, leading to **voter fatigue**.
- It can prove a blunt instrument to deal with complex problems — are voters always the best informed when it comes to making difficult judgements? Who wouldn't want both to cut local taxes and increase spending in areas such as schools?
- Frequent use of direct democracy undermines the whole notion of representative government.
- Recall elections are often motivated by party political factors (e.g. sore losers) rather than genuine questions of ethics or personal misconduct.

Term limits Laws to limit the number of times an elected official can seek re-election. They apply to state-level office only and frequently involve a maximum of two consecutive four-year terms in office.

Exam tip

If debating the pros and cons of direct democracy, make sure you refer to all the main formats and not just the most prominent, i.e. ballot propositions.

Why do Americans vote the way they do?

Vital to understanding this topic is making a distinction between **voter profile** and **political campaigns**. A large number of American voters will always vote for the same party or if seriously disillusioned with 'their' party might abstain. This is due to their **partisan alignment** which in turn normally relates to factors such as gender, race, religious practice, age, geography and wealth. This equates to voter profile. The other major factor, that of the campaign, issues and personalities of the candidates, has already been touched on earlier in this topic. These factors will normally influence **independent** or **non-aligned** voters in how they cast their vote.

Voter profile

Who you are, your background and beliefs will often explain which party you vote for. This is true in both British and American politics. There are a few subtle differences of which you ought to be aware, however. In the USA, race and religion remain far more important indicators of voting behaviour than in Britain. Also the gender gap is more pronounced, and poorer areas do not automatically vote for the less conservative political party. For example, the poorest areas in Britain, such as the North East and South Wales, traditionally vote Labour. By contrast, in the USA, while poor areas of inner cities vote Democrat, the two poorest states — Mississippi and West Virginia — are nowadays Republican strongholds. What aspects of voter profile are therefore vital to grasp?

- **Race**: racial minorities such as African-Americans, Hispanics/Latinos and Asians overwhelmingly vote Democrat. Obama secured in excess of 90% of the African-American vote in both elections he fought, while Clinton managed to secure 88% of the black vote and 65% of both the Asian and Latino vote in 2016. Trump, by contrast, won 58% of the white vote.
- **Religion:** those who attend church regularly are much more likely to vote Republican. In 2016, 81% of white evangelical/'born again' Christians backed Trump, as did 60% of white Catholics. By contrast, 68% of those who had no religious affiliation voted Democrat.
- **Gender**: traditionally, Democrats secure more of the female vote, while Republicans do better among men. In 2016, 54% of women voted for Hillary Clinton (1% less than voted for Obama in 2012) while 53% of men voted for Donald Trump.
- **Age:** younger voters in recent years have voted Democrat while older voters plump more for the Republicans. The figures from 2016 suggest that 56% of those aged 18–24 supported Clinton while Trump enjoyed the support of 53% of those aged over 50. It is worth remembering that older voters are those most likely to vote and younger voters the least likely.
- **Income:** the general picture is that Democrats enjoy greater support among lower-income households, but when it comes to middle- and higher-income groups the parties are more finely balanced. For example, in 2016 Clinton won 53% of the vote among households with an income of less than $30,000 pa (down 10% on the 2012 figure for Obama) while Trump enjoyed a narrow lead among households earning more than $250,000 pa, 48% to 46%.

When coming to conclusions about voting behaviour patterns, it is important to remember that the more boxes a voter 'ticks' in their profile, the more likely they are to vote for one party rather than another. Thus, a young female African-American on a low income is extremely likely to vote Democrat. If, however, the voter is aged 60, white, with no religious affiliation and on a high income, their voting behaviour would be harder to predict with certainty.

> **Exam tip**
>
> When answering a question about voting behaviour, it is always best to use figures from the most recent elections to support your case. Also, when discussing race, make it clear that African-Americans are the most cohesive voting bloc, while Hispanics are much less so, due in part to their diversity. Cuban Americans in Florida, for example, have long voted Republican.

Significance

Voter profile tells us quite a lot about how likely it is that Americans will vote for one party rather than the other, but this needs to be treated carefully. Issues such as where someone lives, whether they own a gun and their political outlook (conservative, liberal, middle of the road, etc.) also come into play. In addition, voters can and do shift their allegiance as well as deciding to abstain. Trump in 2016, for example, won over largish numbers of white lower-income voters without a university education in certain key states such as Michigan.

Parties and their core voting coalitions

As seen above, each party has clear groups among voters that form part of its core. In summary, it could be said that Democrats rely especially on the votes of minorities, younger voters, women (especially educated and unmarried ones) and those with generally progressive social views. They also tend to do well with urban voters and those without strong religious beliefs. By contrast, Republicans do best among older, white, married voters, especially those who are regular churchgoers. Traditionally, the white, unionised blue-collar section of the workforce was reliably Democrat, but this has more recently been a weaker link. Such voters, loosely termed **Reagan Democrats**, first voted Republican in the 1980s and have done so more intermittently since. There is evidence from polling to suggest that Trump did well with this group in 2016, especially in the 'rustbelt' states such as Ohio and Michigan.

Significance

These voter coalitions mean that the parties must tailor their policy platforms carefully to take account of each group's particular concerns. Therefore Democrats can normally be relied upon to be supportive of minority rights and immigration reform, along with a pro-choice position on abortion. The Republicans, by contrast, are supportive of a greater role for (Christian) religion in public life such as prayers in state schools, are pro-life in the abortion debate and favour defending traditional family values. A problem for both parties is keeping their voting coalitions together while also reaching out to new voters. This is especially a concern for the Republicans as the country becomes increasingly racially diverse. Recently, they have sought to broaden their appeal with Hispanic voters, though with mixed results. Appealing overmuch to angry, white, older men is unlikely to win nationwide elections in the medium term, especially in states such as Arizona with a rapidly growing Hispanic population. Equally, the Democrats cannot afford to lose too much of their white-blue-collar support in the rustbelt.

Knowledge check 25

Why do Democrats enjoy more support among women and ethnic minority groups?

Two case studies in voting behaviour

The specification requires that you can quote specific examples from an historic (pre-1980) election and a recent (1980 and afterwards) election that demonstrate factors that affect voting behaviour in practice. You are free to refer to any election, of course, but the examples below may be helpful summaries of two important elections.

1968 presidential election

This was between Republican Richard Nixon (who had lost in 1960) and Democrat Hubert Humphrey. It also witnessed a strong showing from a breakaway Democrat and pro-segregation candidate George Wallace, who won five states in the Deep South, the last third-party or independent candidate to win any ECV. It is considered a re-aligning election for a number of reasons.

First, it marked the end of the Democrats' New Deal Coalition, as conservative white southerners became disaffected by the national party's support for black civil rights. As President Johnson admitted, Democrat support for civil rights was effectively 'signing away the South'. In 1968, many of these white southerners would vote for Wallace; in 1972 and beyond, many would vote Republican.

By contrast, it marked the first major successes for Nixon's 'southern strategy', in other words deliberately targeting those alienated conservative southerners by promising to strengthen law and order in the wake of several serious riots in inner cities, such as the 1965 Watts riots, and some violent anti-war protests.

The election also represented one of the greatest reversals in electoral fortunes. The Democrats had won in 1964 by a landslide, due in part to the legacy of JFK's assassination and in part to the Republicans selecting Barry Goldwater, an ultra-conservative who alienated many moderate voters. By 1968, with a more mainstream candidate and a Democrat presidency scarred by the Vietnam War, among other issues, it was an open race. The Democrats were weakened by serious divisions within their ranks, especially over the Vietnam War. Their 1968 convention in Chicago was marred by serious unrest and the party was divided between anti-war elements led by Senator Eugene McCarthy.

In addition, issues and leadership played a major role. As mentioned above, the unpopularity of the Vietnam War was at its peak. The war had been escalated under the Democrat presidency of Lyndon Johnson but had failed to achieve much tangible success. LBJ had withdrawn from running again and it was difficult for Humphrey, his vice president, to appear credible in offering fresh leadership to resolve issues connected with the war. Nixon, by contrast, could offer this and proved to be the most effective 'agent of change', much as Obama could in 2008, again in the wake of a prolonged and unsatisfactory foreign war.

Finally, it heralded a Republican dominance of the White House for much of the next 40 years when they went on to win 7 out of 10 presidential elections. The only two successful Democrats in that period, Jimmy Carter and Bill Clinton, were both from the South. Losing the South and its Electoral College votes cost the Democrats dearly.

2016 presidential election

As well as being a very recent election, 2016 will go down in the political annals as one of the most significant and surprising. It represented the first time a presidential election had been won by a candidate without political or military experience — Trump could not claim to have a record of public or patriotic service behind him. It also saw a victory for what might be termed populist or anti-establishment politics; indeed, the Democratic nomination came close to being won by Senator Bernie Sanders, the closest the US Senate has to a socialist. It also saw unparalleled levels of personal vitriol and abuse — US politics is often pretty rough and ready, but many observers felt it had reached new depths as Trump in particular called his fellow Republican challengers for the nomination names such as 'Lying Ted' and 'Cry baby Rubio'. He called his opponent 'Crooked Hillary' and suggested she should be in prison.

Some of the key points worth noting in this unusual election include those below.

The issues and slogans raised by Trump, such as 'Make America Great Again', promising a wall with Mexico and re-negotiating some free trade deals, resonated strongly with certain voters. Despite the fact that they were often 'fact-lite', they proved more attractive than 'I'm With Her' or 'Stronger Together'. Clinton found it much easier to highlight flaws and impracticalities in Trump's platform than to project an appealing vision of her own.

Both candidates endured considerable upsets along the way: Trump was seriously harmed by the release of a recording showing him making crude and sexualised comments about women to TV presenter Billy Bush. Clinton, meanwhile, suffered a health scare early in the campaign after a public stumble, followed by recuperation for pneumonia, and in the closing days was hit by a reopening of an FBI investigation into her use of a private email server while Secretary of State. Many Americans felt equally underwhelmed by either candidate: did Clinton have the stamina and good judgement to be president? Did Trump have the temperament and moral dignity? Perhaps it is no surprise that third-party candidates did better than for a while, securing around 5% of the vote.

There were also some unexpected outcomes regarding how different sections of the electorate voted. Clinton, despite being the first woman presidential candidate from a major party, did less well among female voters than Obama. Trump, ironically, did slightly better among Hispanic voters (up 2% to 29%) than Romney had in 2012, despite well-publicised comments referring to Mexican immigrants as rapists and criminals. Also, despite his absence of a conventional religious background, the thrice-married Trump secured a higher percentage of the white evangelical vote than the last Republican candidate. This is perhaps a reminder that voter profiles are not that simple when it comes to making assumptions. For example, women may not always be more attracted to a female candidate who unashamedly stands on a pro-choice platform.

Trump, along with his political inexperience, made no bones about keeping his distance from the Republican political establishment. This led some senior Republicans such as the Bush family to withhold formal endorsement of him. Indeed, Trump made a virtue out of his outsider status, boasting of how he was free of the 'shackles' of party. Never in a recent political campaign has a mainstream candidate run such an independent campaign. In a year when 'experts' were similarly disregarded in the UK's EU referendum, the same happened to an extent in the USA.

Trump won primarily due to the impact his message and strategy (and his opponent's flaws) had on the rustbelt states such as Wisconsin and Michigan. They swung behind him, albeit by small margins, giving him crucial additional Electoral College votes. He also managed to hold on to the Republican base elsewhere and win one or two other swing states such as North Carolina and Florida.

Finally, before one assumes that Trump played the better hand, it needs to be recorded that Clinton arguably lost the election by failing to enthuse the Democrat base as effectively as Obama had done, especially women, youth and African-Americans. Also, one should remember that she won a clear majority of the popular vote, as mentioned earlier in the Electoral College section. The election highlighted the fact that while the Republicans face a demographic problem, the Democrats face a geographical one — too many of their supporters are concentrated in large metropolitan areas and on the east and west coasts. Such a situation does not play well with the current Electoral College set-up.

Why do some Americans not vote or split their votes?

Despite numerous opportunities to vote (or arguably in part, because of that), voter turnout in America remains among the lowest in western democracies. For example, in 2016 only 59% of those eligible actually turned out to vote, around the same as in 2012 (58%), and below the 62% who voted in 2008, which was itself the highest since

Knowledge check 26

Why did the Electoral College system work against Hillary Clinton in 2016?

the 1960s. Turnout is even lower in primaries and local elections. By contrast, turnout in the 2015 British general election was 66%, while that for the 2016 EU referendum was more than 72%. What factors explain why turnout in US elections is so low despite efforts to boost it, such as the Help America Vote Act of 2002 and laws passed during the civil rights era of the 1960s that aimed to promote voting among black Americans?

Reasons why voter turnout is low in the USA

Voter registration and ballot laws vary considerably across the country. Only North Dakota does not require prior registration; everywhere else, voters must actively register to vote. In the UK, the process is compulsory and undertaken nationally by the Electoral Commission; in the USA it is the responsibility of the individual. Many simply do not bother to register in the first place.

Some would argue that the sheer number and campaign frenzy of US elections paradoxically alienates or switches off many voters. This is known as **democratic overload**. Another factor is lack of choice: given the two-party dominance of American politics and a FPTP electoral system, independents and third parties stand little chance of electoral success. This in turn discourages their potential supporters from turning out as they feel their votes will be wasted or they will end up voting instead for a party or candidate for whom they have limited support.

Gerrymandering and the voting history of many states mean that a lot of races are uncompetitive. In a contest where the result is a foregone conclusion, what is the incentive to vote other than civic duty? Some argue that low turnout is a symptom of a wider disillusion with traditional representative politics. In 2016, for example, many ordinary voters were unhappy with both of the main candidates. Turnout in some key swing states such as Ohio and Wisconsin actually fell in 2016 by 4% and 3% respectively. The evidence suggests that many probably Democrat voters failed to be enthused by Clinton's candidature: they disliked her more than being determined to stop Trump.

Also in recent years there has been a trend, especially in some Republican-governed states such as North Carolina, to tighten voter ID laws in the interests of combatting voter fraud. The criteria for acceptable ID (such as driving licences or passports) has been said to disadvantage disproportionately likely Democrat voters, not least from ethnic minorities who are statistically less likely to possess such photo ID.

Significance

Low voter turnout could be said to weaken the mandates of successful candidates in US elections. It also provides insight into the alienation from politics experienced by many Americans who feel that the current range of viable candidates and parties does not adequately represent them. Perhaps it also suggests a cynicism that whoever wins, nothing much changes — politics remains dominated by politicians perceived as motivated by self-interest and in thrall to the special interests of the rich and powerful. Finally, low turnout incentivises candidates to 'get out the vote' as much as trying to change the minds of those certain to vote. Arguably, Trump won in 2016 as much because his opponent failed to mobilise some of her own base sufficiently as because of his own appeal or ability to change voters' minds.

Splitting their vote

It used to be quite common for Americans to split their vote between candidates of different parties. That might mean, for example, voting for a Republican as president but Democrat candidates for Congress. This phenomenon, known as **split-ticket voting**, in part explained why Republican Ronald Reagan enjoyed two strong presidential election results (he won 49 out of 50 states in 1984) yet often faced a Democrat-controlled Congress. It is the opposite of **straight-ticket voting** that is now much more prevalent. Some reasons why voters might split their vote include:

■ In a political system that is more candidate focused, voters may simply be expressing a preference based on personality and political experience as much as on political party.

■ The importance of incumbency, discussed earlier, means that regional political realignment took some while to come about fully. For example, the South had swung decisively behind the Republicans in presidential elections by the 1980s, but Democrats continued to win many congressional races for far longer, typically due to the re-election of longstanding and popular Democrat incumbents. Once they retired or were eventually defeated, their successor was a Republican.

■ Voters like to keep a balance in party control between the different branches of government, namely the executive and the legislature. They actively desire checks and balances and want to avoid one party becoming too powerful. Evidence for this is hard to find, though, so it is not a particularly compelling argument.

Recent developments in split-ticket voting

You need to be aware that split-ticket voting has declined considerably in recent elections — 2016 was the first election in US history when not a single state split its Senate vote. That is to say, every winning Republican senator was to be found in a state that voted for Donald Trump and every victorious Democrat senator stood in a state that also backed Hillary Clinton. By contrast, as recently as 1984 and 1988, just over half of states split their Senate ticket. The picture applies equally to House districts, where nowadays only a handful (26/435 in 2012) split their tickets. Why is this the case?

■ The two main parties are becoming more polarised and homogenous. There are fewer moderates in either, so there is less incentive to split one's vote. In that sense they are becoming narrower and more like Westminster parties.

■ The geographical political realignment is finally complete in most of the country. Thus the South is now Republican in both presidential and congressional elections. After the 2014 mid-terms, other than congressmen in majority-minority districts there was not one Democrat in Congress from the Deep South.

Knowledge check 27

What is the impact of less split-ticketing on the composition of Congress?

Exam tip

It is worth mentioning that there was some split-ticketing in the 2016 election. Vermont, for example, voted overwhelmingly for Clinton over Trump yet returned a Republican governor, Phil Scott, in the same election. Examples such as this suggest we cannot be too emphatic about the demise of split-ticket voting.

How do the UK and the USA compare in terms of campaign finance and electoral systems?

This major topic contains some of the key differences between politics in the USA and the UK, though there are some similarities as well. Areas of similarity include:

- Both systems make use of a majoritarian electoral system, though in the UK many important elections outside those at Westminster make use of other systems, primarily the Additional Member System (AMS).
- Voting behaviour is a product of a variety of factors, with voter profiles and issues playing a major role.
- There are concerns over levels of political participation, most notably in election turnout.

The differences are perhaps the most significant, however. Among the key areas that separate the two political systems are:

- The greater number and regularity of elections in America and the direct election of the head of the executive, a role which in the UK goes to the leader of the winning party in elections for the legislature.
- The use of primaries and caucuses to select candidates in the USA, a role traditionally undertaken in the UK by political parties.
- Election campaigns in America are more candidate focused, with much campaign material omitting any mention of party, although nearly every successful candidate is affiliated with either the Democrats or the Republicans.
- The absence of the facility in the US for a national referendum, but in contrast to the UK, the opportunity in many states for voters to place measures directly on the ballot via ballot initiatives.
- Elections cost vastly more in America and such expenditure is much harder to regulate and limit. The USA tries to limit donations, while in the UK the focus is on capping overall expenditure. For example, in the run-up to the 2015 general election, British parties contesting every seat were limited to spending a total of £19.5 million and individual candidates to an average of just under £40,000. In addition, TV ads cannot be freely purchased. The First Amendment also makes possible reform more problematic in the USA.
- In terms of voter profile, race and religion are far more important as voting determinants in the USA, while class remains a (decreasingly) useful indicator in the UK.
- Turnout is markedly lower in the USA, in part because of the more complex and variable requirements for voter registration.

Finally, it might be worth noting that reforms and changes to electoral systems, campaign finance, etc. are far easier in Britain than in the USA where not only are there powerful vested interests, such as wealthy pressure groups opposed to many changes, but also the additional hurdle of the US Supreme Court.

Knowledge check 28

In what ways are laws concerning political advertising different in the USA compared with the UK?

Summary

By the end of this section, you should know and understand:

■ The frequency of and electoral system used for the main elections in the USA.

■ How candidates are chosen.

■ The role and significance of the party conventions.

■ How the Electoral College works and the controversy surrounding it.

■ The main factors that determine the outcome of elections.

■ Why campaign finance is so difficult to reform.

■ The different forms direct democracy takes in the USA and the associated advantages and drawbacks.

■ The importance of voter profile as well as other factors in determining why Americans vote as they do.

■ How one historic and one recent election can be used to illustrate changes in voting behaviour.

■ Why relatively few Americans vote.

■ What is meant by split-ticket voting and why it has declined recently.

You should also be aware of some of the ways that the electoral process and direct democracy impact on other parts of US government and politics. This is known as the **synoptic** element.

■ The indirect election of the president and biennial elections and the resultant 'constant campaigning' highlight some key flaws of the US Constitution **(The constitutional frameworks of US government)**.

■ Voting behaviour highlights the core groups of supporters for each main party **(Political parties)**.

■ The importance of primaries weakens a key function of political parties **(Political parties)**.

■ Candidates often receive political donations from pressure groups sympathetic to their position **(Pressure groups)**.

■ The Supreme Court has been a key reason why campaign finance reform has not been more successful **(The judicial branch of government: the Supreme Court)**.

■ Political parties

How are the two main parties organised and structured?

The previous section should already give you many clues about the nature of political parties in the USA. They are weaker and less centralised than in the UK, as election campaigns are more candidate centred. Individuals are largely responsible for raising campaign funds themselves and adopting their own policy platforms to win both the primary stage and the 'real' election. There are plenty of instances of candidates running virtually as independents, Trump being the most notable recent example. Yet American politics remains dominated by the two main parties and those parties have become much more **polarised and partisan** in recent years. They increasingly resemble the clearly distinct blocs that we associate with UK parties. So what points are still valid about how US parties are structured?

Parties are organised on a state basis, which often have their own rules, for example how they award delegates in primary elections. Arguably there are not two but 100 main parties in America.

They both have a national coordinating body, the RNC (Republican National Committee) and the DNC (Democratic National Committee), with a single chair, who in 2017 was Ronna McDaniel for the RNC and Tom Perez for the DNC. But these posts are not the equivalent of the party leader in the UK, they are more akin to the roles of party chairs, being more of a coordinating and administrative role. Nor are they necessarily stepping stones to further promotion, though the previous chair of the RNC, Reince Priebus, was initially chosen by Trump as his chief of staff though was forced out after six months.

The national party bodies generally stay neutral in primary contests, though Debbie Schultz resigned as DNC chair in 2016 when allegations were made that the DNC tried to influence the primary outcome to help Clinton defeat Sanders.

US parties retain an element of the '**big tent**' about them, that is to say they contain a wide range of views despite the parties becoming more clearly defined over the past 20 years or so. This generally reflects the diversity of the country, not least by geography. Thus, white Democrats running in the South are more likely to be pro-gun and pro-life than Democrats elsewhere. Republicans in the North East are more likely to adopt a moderate platform than **GOP** candidates elsewhere. For example, the three most liberal House Republicans in 2013 came from either New York or Pennsylvania, while the two most conservative Democrats came from Georgia and Oklahoma — interestingly, both the latter have since been replaced by Republicans.

The divisions within each party are perhaps best reflected by membership of congressional caucuses such as the Blue Dog Coalition by fiscally conservative Democrats or the Freedom Caucus by the most conservative House Republicans. The divisions among Republicans in Congress over a replacement for Obamacare in 2017 also highlighted internal party divisions. Trump's plan went too far for some and not far enough for others. Incidentally this also revealed the weakness of a president's control over their own party even in the 'honeymoon' period of the presidency.

GOP An abbreviation for the Grand Old Party, a frequently used nickname for the Republican Party.

Knowledge check 29

How much power do central party bodies have in US politics?

What are the main differences between the two main US parties in both their platforms and core support?

The core support for each party has already been alluded to in the section on voting behaviour, but as a brief summary:

- Republican core supporters tend to be white, older, religious, wealthier and less keen on socially liberal policies such as gay rights. Most favour lower taxes and less money spent on welfare benefits. Some may well be climate change sceptics and not prioritise environmental controls. They also tend to champion the rights of gun owners and a hawkish foreign policy that is tough on perceived threats to America's security, whether that be the USSR during the Cold War or Islamist terrorism since 2001. They are also staunch supporters of Israel. They are more likely to live in rural, small-town or prosperous suburbs and watch Fox News.
- Democrat core supporters could be said to be the polar opposites in many ways. They are more likely to be from ethnic minorities, younger, socially liberal and supporters of causes such as women's and LGBT rights. They are less likely to be deeply religious and more concerned with proper support for the neediest in society, hence their support for measures such as Obamacare. They will place a higher priority on green measures and favour working with international bodies in

global affairs and trying, where possible, to lessen tension via diplomacy — witness Obama's efforts in his second term to achieve better relations with Cuba and Iran. Most will want stricter gun laws and are more likely to live in large cosmopolitan urban areas, especially on either coast, and to watch MSNBC.

The platforms of each party both explain and reflect these groups of core supporters. Some of the key policy differences are outlined in the table.

Policy area	Democrat	Republican
Obamacare	Support	Reject
Prioritise cutting taxes and reducing the size of federal government	Oppose: federal government can help provide better opportunities for less advantaged Americans	Support: federal government tends to waste taxpayers' money
Have a greater place for religion in public life	Oppose: not because they are anti religion but they prefer to retain the church/state separation	Support: in part due to strong ties with the religious right
Commit the USA to signing up to global protocols to reduce carbon emissions	Support: climate change and the environment are crucial issues for all	Oppose: many are sceptical of global warming; keen on energy security and maximising US ability to exploit its natural resources
Strongly favour protecting and enhancing the rights of discriminated/minority groups such as women, ethnic minorities and the LGBT community	Support: not surprisingly given their voter base	Oppose: mainly due to socially conservative views on the family, but unlikely to reverse most existing anti-discrimination laws
Immigration reform, allowing some illegal immigrants to acquire citizenship	Support: again not least because of their support from ethnic minorities	Oppose: build a wall!
Support for Israel	Conditional support: favour a two-state solution with a proper voice for Palestinians	Largely unconditional support: Israel is seen as America's only true ally in an unstable part of the world

How have US political parties developed in recent times?

In the not so recent past, political scientists often made three key points about US parties:

■ They were broad, catch-all and '**big tent**' parties, i.e. they contained a lot of diversity within them, arguably as great sometimes as the differences between them.

■ Parties as institutions were in decline in the USA. Hence in 1972 David Broder wrote a book entitled *The Party's Over*, which was in part a plea for a reinvigoration of the party system, less split-ticket voting and 'some unvarnished political partisanship'.

■ US parties were essentially un-ideological. Their names were interchangeable: both believed in democracy and in a republican form of government. This contrasts with the UK where the party labels — Conservative, Liberal Democrat, UKIP, etc. — clearly convey a set of values and broad ideology by their names alone.

These three statements can safely be said to be no longer key truths or assumptions. The reality is often what is termed '**hyper-partisanship**', especially in Congress — unwillingness to work together 'across the aisle' and work together in a bipartisan manner. The new political landscape could be summarised as:

■ two parties with very different core groups of supporters and clearly defined policy differences (see table above), which reflect contrasting values or ideologies. The parties are more homogenous and united in Congress, with fewer centrists or moderates in either camp.

There is increased partisanship when it comes to voting in Congress. For example, in the Obama years, not a single Republican in either chamber voted in favour of Obamacare. Equally, in the wake of several shooting tragedies such as at Sandy Hook and San Bernardino, only a handful of senators from either side went against the bulk of their party when voting on gun-control measures.

This polarisation is also seen in confirmation votes for Supreme Court justices. While near unanimous votes used to be quite common, the most recent ones have been much more partisan. For example, when Elena Kagan was confirmed in 2010, the vote was 63–37, with only 4 Republicans backing her. Senate Republicans also successfully blocked Obama's attempts in 2016 to nominate a successor to Antonin Scalia. Likewise, many other Senate confirmation votes reflect a strict party divide. Trump's choice of Rex Tillerson as Secretary of State scraped through the Senate Foreign Relations committee in 2017 by a margin of just 11–10, with every Republican supporting him (including Trump's bitter rival in the primaries, Marco Rubio) and every Democrat opposing him.

There is also some evidence of attempts towards greater centralisation and coordination of the party structures. Back in 1994, then Speaker of the House, Republican Newt Gingrich, helped draw up the 'Contract with America', a list of eight reforms and ten bills that Republicans would implement if they won control of Congress. The pledge was signed by nearly all Republican candidates. The Democrats in part responded with their 'Six for 06' agenda in 2006. The central party organisations such as the DNC and RNC, as well as the parties' groupings in Congress, also try to channel funding into key elections races they see as competitive, not least to 'shore up' vulnerable incumbents. In essence, recent years have seen **party renewal** rather than **party decline**.

Nevertheless, one does need to be careful about seeing US parties as now identical to their UK counterparts, namely two largely monolithic adversarial groups. As a result of the primary system and candidate-focused nature of much political campaigning, parties still remain weaker. Also, there remain examples of votes in Congress where legislators will break ranks with the majority of their party colleagues. When the Senate voted to build the Keystone XL pipeline in January 2015, 9 Democrats voted alongside all 53 Republicans. Several of these were senators from 'red states' such as North Dakota (Heidi Heitkamp) and West Virginia (Joe Manchin). Note, too, that 'blue states' can still elect Republican politicians to state-wide office and vice versa.

Exam tip

The selection of Donald Trump as GOP candidate is a good example to use of how weak party establishments/ structures still are in influencing candidate selection.

Hence in 2016, Democrat John Bel Edwards won the governorship of Louisiana while Republican Chris Sununu became governor of New Hampshire, a state where the GOP lost both the presidential and the Senate race. Some aspects of the US political map remain 'purple'. The comment by former House Speaker Tip O'Neill, that 'all politics is local', still has plenty of currency in it.

Significance

The growth of polarisation has, among many other things, made it much harder to get some laws through Congress and limited the president's 'power to persuade'. There is little incentive for deal-making, and at its worse it can lead to a shutdown of the federal government, as happened for more than two weeks in October 2013 when the parties could not agree on the budget. It has also increased the level of hostility and vitriol in political discourse. Many Republicans questioned Obama's constitutional qualifications even to be president ('birther movement'), while in January 2017, veteran Democrat congressman John Lewis described Trump as an illegitimate president. Finally, polarisation has in turn probably alienated many moderate Americans, put off by the language and approach of many politicians and the two Americas, red and blue, they claim to represent.

Knowledge check 30

What is meant by the term 'purple America'?

Why is the USA dominated by two parties?

There is no doubt that, unlike contemporary Britain, America remains an overwhelmingly two-party political system. In 2017 there were no independents in the House, both independent senators caucus with the Democrats (usually vote along similar lines to them) and one of them (Bernie Sanders) sought the Democrat presidential nomination in 2016; there was also only one independent governor, Bill Walker in Alaska. In the 2016 presidential election, third-party candidates mustered barely 5% of the overall vote. By contrast, third parties play a large role in UK politics, with several parties being represented at Westminster, including the SNP with more than 30 MPs even after the 2017 general election and UKIP, which won the largest number of MEP seats in the 2014 European elections. This raises the questions: why are independents and third parties so weak in America and why do the two parties remain dominant?

- The electoral system is majoritarian (FPTP), which discriminates against third-party candidates and can lead to the 'wasted vote' syndrome. Even with 19% of the popular vote in 1992, independent candidate Ross Perot received not a single Electoral College vote.
- The complexity and often cost of ballot access laws can make it very hard for candidates not from one of the two big parties to get enough nomination signatures even to get on the ballot in all 50 states. Thus Green Party candidate Jill Stein failed to get on the ballot in three states (including Nevada) in 2016.
- The US parties remain quite broad and reflect regional differences. Also, the primary system enables outsiders to run, albeit adopting a party label. Donald Trump is again perhaps the classic example. Choice within parties to an extent precludes choice between a range of parties.

- Attractive policies of third parties and independents are often 'co-opted' by one or other of the main parties. The success of George Wallace in 1968 in attracting conservative white southerners led the Republicans to develop policies that resonated with them in subsequent years. Similarly, in 1992, Ross Perot's focus on reducing the budget deficit was later picked up by the main parties.
- Their candidates are often labelled as extremists. Republicans in 1968 attacked Wallace, saying, 'If you liked Hitler, you'll love Wallace.'
- Third parties and independents are largely ignored by the mainstream. This creates something of a vicious circle, as without publicity it remains hard for them to achieve recognition and thus they remain largely ignored by the media. Candidates need to have an average poll rating of 15% to qualify for the televised presidential debates.
- With finance and funding being so important in US elections, again third parties and independents find themselves disadvantaged. Few major donors want to contribute to candidates whom they see as having little chance of success. It is noteworthy that the last independent to make any significant impact on a presidential election, Ross Perot, was a billionaire who largely self-funded.

In what ways do political parties differ in the UK and the USA?

This is an area where the UK/USA contrast remains strong, despite a growing similarity as US parties became more distinct from the 1980s and the main UK parties became more centrist from the late 1990s and the emergence of New Labour. The key remaining differences include:

- US parties remain broader and more decentralised, in part due to the sheer size and diversity of the country.
- The UK party system in recent times has become much more of a multiparty system, not least in the regions but also with the existence of a coalition government from 2010 to 2015. US politics, by contrast, remains dominated at every level by two parties.
- Third parties and independents remain largely impotent in America, except sometimes for their 'spoiling power' in tight races. Arguably, the Green Party's candidate in 2000, Ralph Nader, siphoned off enough votes in Florida to deny Democrat candidate Al Gore victory there and thus hand the whole election to George W. Bush.
- UK parties have clear leaders (chosen ultimately by a nationwide ballot of members) and manifestoes, while the US parties have no direct equivalent, although policy platforms have become increasingly uniform in both parties of late. Also, the absence of nationwide primary elections in the UK gives more power to the party machines, both local and national.
- Levels of party discipline in the respective legislatures remain higher in the UK than in the USA. This is despite Westminster backbenchers becoming more rebellious (e.g. Cameron's coalition government being defeated in the vote on air strikes on Syria in August 2013) and more cohesive voting by party in Congress.

Summary

By the end of this section, you should know and understand:

- How US parties are structured and some of the remaining differences and factions within them.
- How US parties differ in their core platforms and voter blocs.
- The recent developments in US parties, especially the rise in partisanship and polarisation.
- How and why third parties and independents remain marginalised in US politics.
- The key differences between US and UK parties in terms of organisation, leadership and voting behaviour in the legislatures.

You should also be aware of some of the ways that the electoral process and direct democracy impact on other parts of US government and politics. This is known as the **synoptic** element.

- How weak political parties increase the focus on candidate-centred campaigning **(The electoral process and direct democracy)**.
- The growing partisanship in Congress makes it harder for a president to make deals with and persuade more moderate legislators if a different party to that of the president controls Congress **(The executive branch of government: president)**.
- The party leaderships play an increasing role in Congress where, especially in the House, the two groups much more closely resemble Westminster parties. There is also increased use of the filibuster and party unity in voting **(The legislative branch of government: Congress)**.
- Growing partisanship is shown in recent Senate confirmation hearings for Supreme Court justices **(The judicial branch of government: the Supreme Court)**.

■ Pressure groups

What do we mean by political pluralism in the USA?

As one of the most diverse democracies in the world, there is a huge range of political views and interests in the USA. In essence, this is what we mean by the term **political pluralism**. The term also pre-supposes that democracy is made up of competing influences and interest groups. Although dominated by two main parties, and sharing a common commitment to notions of American values such as liberty, opportunity and justice, in reality there are numerous often competing viewpoints that seek to influence decision makers in DC and all 50 states. For example, while every American reveres the concept of 'freedom', citizens interpret it in hugely different ways. To racial minorities such as African-Americans, it is about the freedom to be treated fairly by the police and the absence of discrimination; for conservative (and perhaps especially some of white) America, it is about the freedom to retain most of one's wealth (low taxes) and the freedom to enjoy property and possessions, not least guns, without fear of confiscation or interference by the government; for big business such as Wall Street banks, it is about the freedom to operate with the minimum of government regulation; for consumers, it is about the right to purchase products that are safe and accurately advertised.

These different interpretations of freedom (and indeed of other US values), along with the country's racial, regional, religious and cultural diversity, explain the strength and significance of pressure groups. Strong pressure groups are one of the main consequences of US political pluralism.

What are the different categories of pressure groups in the USA?

As with any democracy, including the UK, the fundamental aim of US pressure groups is identical: to influence policy at all levels in the interests of their cause, and to protect their members from unwelcome policies and laws. Traditionally, though, all pressure groups are classified by both membership/aims and status.

Membership and aims

Pressure groups are traditionally grouped as **interest/sectional** groups or **cause/promotional** groups depending on their membership and aims.

Interest groups seek to defend and advance their own members. Examples in the US include labour unions such as the National Education Association (NEA), which is the largest teaching union with nearly 3 million members, or the National Association of Realtors (estate agents), which is a trade association with more than 1 million members.

Cause groups aim to promote broader causes which they consider as beneficial/right for society as a whole. Their motivation might be described as more altruistic and less selfish than that of interest groups. Examples of key cause groups include the Children's Defense Fund, which promotes the rights and well-being of children, and the League of Conservation Voters, which lobbies for a pro-environment agenda by state and federal governments.

These definitions are not entirely helpful, however, as many pressure groups combine elements of both categories and are known as **hybrid groups**. For example, the National Rifle Association seeks to protect interests of its (gun-owning) members but also seeks to promote more widely a defence of the Second Amendment and the role/status of responsible gun ownership in the USA.

Status

Pressure groups can also be classified by their status, especially whether they are **insider** or **outsider** groups. Insider groups are generally said to possess the following attributes:

- close ties with the political establishment (legislators, government departments, etc.)
- greater financial resources and thus they are able to employ paid lobbyists and spend significant amounts at election times
- a reliance on personal contacts, formal and informal meetings with decision makers — much of their work is done in private and behind closed doors
- a greater emphasis generally on opposition to unwelcome change via new laws or regulations rather than majorly changing the status quo
- often a fairly small but select membership
- being routinely consulted by government/legislators on policy and legislation
- a greater likelihood of success in exercising influence.

Pressure groups typically classified as insider groups include business/institutional groups such as the US Chamber of Commerce and the American Farm Bureau

Federation or professional bodies such as the American Bar Association (ABA). Most corporate donors also fall into this category.

Some of the characteristics of outsider groups include:

- often a large, mass membership
- fewer financial resources and a greater reliance on volunteers rather than paid staff, and effective use of social media to promote public awareness
- a lack of strong and established links with existing political institutions such as Congress. Such groups often feel the need to 'make a noise' in order to be listened to
- the use of **direct action**, for instance demonstrations and encampments such as those carried out by the Occupy movement in 2011–12. In some cases this can lead to violence and clashes with the authorities, as with protests loosely associated with the 'Black Lives Matter' movement (although the organisation itself promotes non-violence) in the wake of police shootings of African-Americans in places such as Ferguson, Missouri in 2014
- a strong desire frequently to challenge the status quo and hence the political and business elite — this may be in areas such as economics, environment and race
- a relative lack of routine success in achieving their aims, though some outsider groups such as the civil rights movement (and associated specific pressure groups such as the NAACP) have achieved many of their aims and successfully challenged the political status quo.

The role of pressure groups and PACs/Super PACs in election campaigns and policy making

One of the main differences between pressure groups in the UK and the USA is that in the latter, many groups are actively involved in election campaigns. They will often donate funds via their political action committees (such as the NRA's Victory Fund) to favoured candidates and produce voting guidance, sometimes in the form of scorecards that show candidates' voting records on the area important to that pressure group. Some even specifically rate or endorse certain candidates. The League of Conservation Voters for more than 20 years has produced a 'Dirty Dozen' hit-list of candidates (mainly Republicans) it wants defeated due to their policy/voting record on the environment. In 2016, though, only 4 out of 12 on the list (which included Donald Trump) failed to get elected, which suggests pressure groups are far from all-powerful.

Pressure groups, especially the larger, well-financed ones, are big players in campaign finance raising and spend millions of dollars each election cycle, thus adding to the ever-growing cost of US elections. Outside groups raised more than $600 million in support of the various 2016 presidential candidates via their PACs/Super PACs. Some of this was wealthy individuals, but much of it came via pressure groups. The list of donors on each side says a great deal about the policy positions of the candidates. For example, 87% of agribusiness donations went to Republicans, as did 89% of donations from the energy and oil sector. By contrast, 99% of labour union donations went to Democrats, while EMILY's List, which works for the election of progressive, pro-choice female Democrat candidates, raised and spent around $40 million on favoured candidates such as Tammy Duckworth, elected senator for Illinois in 2016.

Exam tip

It is a good idea to show you are aware that these classifications can be quite loose and fluid. For example, some pressure groups can become more influential/insider when a certain party dominates politics. Thus conservative religious groups such as the Family Research Council can expect to be listened to carefully by Republican administrations.

Knowledge check 32

In what ways can pressure groups influence US elections?

Certain politicians are also more likely to receive donations than others. The link with incumbency is noted below, but those who are chairs or senior figures on powerful and relevant congressional committees can also anticipate hefty donations, especially from corporate donors. For example, Jeb Hensarling, Republican chair of the House Financial Services Committee, received more than $1.1 million in campaign donations from the finance and banking sector in the 2015–16 election cycle.

In addition to election campaigns, many pressure groups become heavily involved in certain ballot initiative campaigns. Thus in 2016, Everytown for Gun Safety, a pro-gun-control group with millions in funding from billionaire Michael Bloomberg, successfully backed the Question 1 ballot initiative in Nevada that eliminated loopholes allowing guns to be sold without background checks online and at gun shows. Equally, in 2008, many conservative religious groups successfully poured money into supporting Prop 8 in California that banned same-sex marriage.

It is a moot point how powerful and influential pressure groups are in election campaigns. In 2016, Trump received relatively few donations from pressure groups yet won the election. Many pro-Republican pressure groups had donated heavily to more establishment candidates in the primaries, such as Jeb Bush and Marco Rubio. Likewise, Clinton received large donations from Democrat-leaning pressure groups via their Super PACs and outspent her Republican rival yet still lost. Pressure groups partly tend to back candidates most likely to win, so in a year of anti-establishment politics, they had less impact on the final outcome. They certainly have an influence on policy, but it tends more to serve as a reinforcement and reminder to politicians of their policy stance. A Democrat from a majority-minority district will already have a strong commitment to civil rights; endorsement from civil rights groups are unlikely to affect it, but will nonetheless act as an additional incentive to keep that issue high on their policy agenda. It would be incorrect to see pressure groups as 'buying' politicians; equally, they are hardly disinterested altruistic donors either.

Knowledge check 33

Why can it not be said that pressure groups can 'buy' votes in Congress?

Pressure groups and incumbents

When assessing the impact of pressure groups on political campaigns and policies, arguably their greatest influence is on reinforcing the re-election of incumbents. PACs have one overriding priority: get the most 'bang for their buck'. Hence business group PACs donate 90% of their campaign funds to incumbents, reaching 98% in the case of the electronics and communications sector. Labour groups also favour incumbents, with 82% of their donations going to those already elected. This suggests that many groups prioritise backing winners and thus securing access to law-makers. Candidates who share a group's outlook and values but are fighting an unwinnable race are unlikely to be the recipients of pressure group largesse. Therefore one consequence of the involvement of pressure groups and their PACs is to reinforce high levels of incumbent re-election for both parties, which reached 98% for the 2016 House elections.

Knowledge check 34

How do US pressure groups bolster the re-election of incumbents?

Pressure groups and political parties

A common question raised by political commentators and indeed examiners is whether pressure groups are more powerful than political parties. There is no simple answer since they both have essentially different functions. Political parties are there to fight and win elections and to provide some political 'spine' to the body politic by organising elected representatives in Congress. They also provide broad(ish) labels under which candidates can run with a recognisable set of principles and a policy platform. Pressure groups, by contrast, seek to influence and keep accountable those in power. Certainly parties as institutions and structures are weaker in the USA than in the UK, and the reverse is true regarding pressure groups.

Yet the relationship between the two often remains close and interdependent. Parties, or more particularly candidates running under their labels, frequently need the campaign funding and endorsements from groups that are relevant and prominent in their state or district. Once in office, they then need to pay close attention to their voting record. Yet pressure groups also rely on elected politicians for much of their influence. They need to be aware that legislators can often have competing forces on them when it comes to voting in Congress: their party leadership, core voters who participate in primaries and the wider electorate. In an anti-establishment atmosphere and one where social media means that political issues and controversies can 'trend' very quickly, many politicians are careful not to be seen (at least too overtly) to be in the pockets of special interest groups. Nevertheless, their natural voting constituency probably means that they will want to adopt policies and a voting record in line with those of supportive pressure groups. In that sense, pressure groups tend to reflect rather than mould the positions of candidates and parties.

Do pressure groups help or harm US democracy?

This is one of the key debates in the topic and one that you need to be fully at ease with. It all revolves around the **elitist versus pluralist** theories of pressure groups. The **elitist theory** proposes that some groups, especially insider ones, are more powerful than others. Their close ties with legislators and powerful resources mean it is an uneven playing field. Many criticise the dominance that special interests (especially business ones) have on government. This is often termed the 'iron triangle', where pressure groups collude with government agencies and key legislators to maintain the status quo and prevent reforms that threaten their interests. Traditionally associated with the defence industry, it has also been linked to the farming lobby. Here, pressure groups such as agricultural businesses (makers of fertiliser, agricultural machinery, etc.) work alongside the US Department of Agriculture and congressmen from states with big agricultural sectors to keep farm subsidies (and hence food prices) artificially high. This benefits the government agency that sees its budget/influence sustained, legislators who receive large donations from agribusinesses, and of course the businesses and farming lobby themselves.

The **pluralist theory** advocates that in a huge and dynamic and evolving democracy, competing pressure groups jostle for power and influence much as political parties do. The best organised and most popular prevail, there are no inevitable outcomes and democracy is fundamentally all about compromise between these competing groups.

What are some of the key arguments put forward as to whether pressure groups help or hinder US democracy?

Representation: they enabled the wide diversities of America to be represented, as well as those with no direct voice: animals, the environment, illegal immigrants, etc. They also allow a broader spectrum of interests to be represented in a way not possible in a rigid two-party system. Critics would argue that the dominance of a few well-connected groups (e.g. Wall Street and the corporate world) means that some interests in the USA are much better represented than others. The establishment prevails at the expense of the ordinary citizen.

Participation: in a nation with low levels of turnout in elections, pressure groups encourage more Americans to become politically engaged and active. They also promote political activity between elections. However, critics would say that only a minority of pressure group members are activists. Many are 'cheque book' members, who join either out of a general sympathy with the aims of the movement but do not wish to get involved further or simply because of the practical benefits bestowed by membership.

Knowledge check 35

How do pressure groups help political participation?

Education and public debate: pressure groups promote public debate and awareness of a whole range of issues that legislators might otherwise ignore. Their literature and campaigns at election times make voters more informed when casting their vote. The counter-argument is that the material put out by pressure groups is necessarily one-sided and biased, and simply adds to the huge volume of campaign propaganda that either confuses voters or reinforces existing attitudes.

What are some of the key differences between UK and US pressure groups?

In many ways, US and UK pressure groups share a great deal in common. The ways they are classified and categorised are pretty similar. Both countries have clear insider and outsider groups as well as hybrid groups. Also their fundamental aim, of influencing decision makers without seeking elected office, is identical. So what are the key differences?

US pressure groups are much more likely to be directly involved in election campaigns by endorsing candidates, making political donations and informing voters about the policy positions of individual candidates. In part this is because election law is different. The First Amendment enables groups to spend money and promote issues in a way that campaign spending limits and rules on television adverts do not in the UK.

There are more **access points** in the USA. Most UK pressure groups have traditionally focused on Westminster and Whitehall (though devolved government and, pre-Brexit, EU membership have altered this somewhat), while US groups target not just Congress and the White House but also state governments where many important decisions are made. In addition, the importance of the Supreme Court means that many groups will provide *amicus curiae* (friends of the court) briefings to the court outlining their arguments on particular cases using legal arguments.

Knowledge check 36

Why are there more access points in the USA compared with the UK?

Some interest groups are more significant and prominent in the USA. For example, the legacies of slavery and civil rights mean that black rights have traditionally enjoyed a higher profile. Equally, religious (specifically conservative evangelical) groups tend to hold more sway 'across the pond'.

The (relatively) lower levels of party unity in the USA give more scope to pressure groups to influence congressmen in how they vote on individual measures. Thus, in traditionally conservative states, especially in the South, even Democrats (few as they are) would be wary of being too emphatically pro-choice or pro-gun control.

Summary

By the end of this section, you should know and understand:

- How and why the USA is a politically pluralist nation and how pressure groups fit into that.
- The different ways in which pressure groups can be categorised and the limitation of these classifications.
- Why insider groups are generally regarded to be more likely to succeed.
- How pressure groups are involved in political campaigns via PACs/Super PACs.
- The main arguments on both sides about whether pressure groups help or hinder democracy.
- The main differences from UK pressure groups.

You should also be aware of some of the ways that the electoral process and direct democracy impact on other parts of US government and politics. This is known as the **synoptic** element.

- US pressure groups often seek to lobby the Supreme Court **(The judicial branch of government: the Supreme Court)**.
- Pressure groups are often broadly aligned with one of the main political parties **(Political parties)**.
- Pressure groups via their PACs/Super PACS often make political donations to individual candidates and get involved directly in ballot initiative campaigns **(The electoral process and direct democracy)**.

■ Civil rights

Key landmarks and factors in the developments of civil rights in America

Americans place a high value on individual rights and liberties. These rights cover a huge spectrum of areas, including race, gender, sexuality, ownership of property and guns, and free speech. This is not surprising, perhaps, given that very soon after the ratification of the Constitution, the first ten amendments were passed in the shape of the **1791 Bill of Rights**. Among the key rights enumerated in that document are:

- freedom of speech and political expression (First Amendment rights)
- the right to bear arms (Second Amendment)
- the right not to incriminate oneself (later interpreted as the right to remain silent under police or judicial questioning: Fifth Amendment or 'Miranda' rights)
- a ban on 'cruel and unusual' punishments (Eighth Amendment).

Also be aware that the Constitution has a 'due process clause' which guarantees equality of treatment under the law to all US citizens.

Since then civil rights have been added to in various ways:

- **Additional constitutional amendments** such as those passed in the immediate aftermath of the Civil War (Fourteenth–Sixteenth Amendments) have given additional rights to Americans, for example equal protection under the law, and banned racial discrimination in granting the vote. The Nineteenth Amendment, meanwhile, gave women full and equal voting rights.
- **Landmark rulings** by the Supreme Court have expanded rights by taking broader and more expansive interpretations of the Bill of Rights. For example, beginning with the famous 1954 *Topeka* v *Brown* case, moves to desegregate schooling have been based upon the Equal Protection clause. The same has been

true of developments to extend rights to gay Americans. The 2003 case *Lawrence v Texas* struck down Texan anti-sodomy laws on that basis, while in 2015 the Supreme Court in *Obergefell* v *Hodges* held that the fundamental right to marry is guaranteed to same-sex couples by both the Due Process Clause and the Equal Protection Clause of the Fourteenth Amendment.

- **Federal laws** passed by Congress arguably have had less impact on the protection of civil rights than landmark judgements. Many key laws were passed during the 1960s, most notably the 1964 Civil Rights Act, the 1965 Voting Rights Acts and the 1963 Equal Pay Act that ended wage differences based on gender. The first two emerged out of the black civil rights movement led by, among others, Martin Luther King.
- **Pressure group action** has also contributed significantly to extending and defending civil rights for a whole range of Americans. These can range from 'conservative' groups that seek to promote the civil rights of the unborn (anti-abortion groups such as the American Life League) to 'progressive' groups (such as the NAACP) that want to defend and enhance the rights of, among others, gays and ethnic minorities. Lobbying Congress and state governments and submitting *amicus curiae* briefs to the Supreme Court all form part of their tactics.

Pressure groups and civil rights

Not surprisingly given both the diversity of the USA and the relatively weak party system, pressure groups are very prominent in the struggle for civil rights on behalf of all kinds of groups. As noted already, the notion of civil rights extends widely and often produces clashes over whose rights prevail. For example, in the abortion debate, some would fight vigorously to defend the civil rights of women over their reproductive rights while others would equally strongly seek to defend the rights of the unborn. It is not surprising, therefore, that nearly all struggles over civil rights involve pressure groups, often on opposing sides. Many pressure groups have successfully championed civil rights, with the NAACP for example often involved in helping to bring cases concerning rights for African-Americans before the courts, by funding much of the legal costs. The American Civil Liberties Union has been prominent in supporting cases such as *Miranda* v *Arizona* and *Engel* v *Vitale* (1962), which banned prayers in state schools, thus defending the rights of Americans not to have religion 'imposed' on them by the state.

Exam tip

This topic fits in very well with some other topics such as pressure groups and the Supreme Court. Make sure you revise/study this material seeing these clear links and be ready to use any examples and points across the relevant topics.

Knowledge check 37

What are the main influences on extending and developing civil rights in the USA?

Case study

How have civil rights developed for gun owners?

The right to bear arms

Among the rights protected in the Bill of Rights, one of the most controversial is the right to bear arms, to own a gun. This is a civil right that is virtually unique to the USA in being specifically protected. While the original intention was for citizens in the young republic to have the right to defend themselves against native Americans and British colonists, it has developed in the last century to become a debate about how far this right should be extended or preserved to individuals for sport

but also for self-defence. Those challenging the untrammelled right of gun owners would point to the following as reasons to restrict this right:

- High levels of gun crime, especially in inner cities. For example, Chicago alone saw 141 murders in 2016.
- Several high-profile mass shootings, such as those at Sandy Hook school in 2012 when 20 children and 6 staff were killed or in 2017 at Fort Lauderdale Airport where 5 people were shot dead.

- The Founding Fathers never intended gun ownership to be an individual right but rather meant it as a right for members of state militias to keep their guns at home in case of an attack.

By contrast, a strong pro-gun lobby headed by the powerful and well-funded National Rifle Association, but also by other groups such as the even more hardline Gun Owners of America, has sought to defend the civil rights of law-abiding gun owners. They would essentially argue that private gun ownership is an inalienable right for all American citizens and that only a tyrannical government would seek to take guns away. Private gun ownership is both a guarantor and a symbol of a truly free people.

This struggle is a classic civil rights clash, pitting the rights of gun owners against those who claim to have a right to live in a society with less gun-related violence. What is the impact of this civil rights battle on politics? It has led to gun control being a position on which most American politicians have to take a public stand in their campaigns. Pressure groups from both sides push candidates to take a stand one way or the other, often awarding them 'ratings' based on their statements and voting record.

It has also meant gun control is often debated in Congress, with measures being passed and repealed according to which party is in the stronger position. For instance, in 1994 Clinton signed into law the Public Safety and Recreational Firearms Use Protection Act, which effectively banned assault rifles for a 10-year period. Yet a Republican president and Congress allowed it to lapse in 2004. It has not been renewed since despite much lobbying from the gun-control lobby.

The right to bear arms has become a key definer of differences between the parties. Most Democrats would nowadays back proposals to tighten up US gun laws, for example banning the sale of the most lethal weapons and demanding tighter background checks on purchasers. By contrast, most Republicans would strongly defend the right to bear arms and many in Congress have opposed even quite minor gun-control measures.

The issue has also ended up in the Supreme Court on occasion, most notably in 2008 with the controversial landmark ruling in *DC* v *Heller* where by a narrow 5–4 majority the Court struck down DC's gun law that generally prohibited carrying a pistol without a licence and also required that all firearms be kept unloaded. The case upheld the Second Amendment protecting an individual's right to possess a firearm unconnected with service in a militia. This ruling was reinforced by the 2010 case *McDonald* v *Chicago*.

Finally, gun control has demonstrated the lack of presidential power on occasion. President Obama in his second term desperately wanted Congress to pass some gun-control measures, but to little avail. Republicans in both houses were largely unwilling to back such moves and without their support nothing happened.

Exam tip

The AQA specification requires you to know about the impact of only one civil rights topic on US politics. You can choose any one you want so it is not compulsory to learn the example given above. If you want to study or research other ones such as race, abortion, sexual orientation or gender, that is fine. Don't study more than one in detail though.

How does campaigning and protecting civil rights differ between the USA and the UK?

As one would expect with western democracies, there are a lot of similarities in the general nature of civil rights in both countries. Each values the rights of minorities and individual liberties in a general sense. Both nations have laws in place as well as other constitutional safeguards to prevent infringement of these rights. However, due to both their constitutions and their political culture and history, there are some differences between them.

US civil rights are much more **entrenched** than those in the UK by being embodied in the US Constitution and its amendments, especially the Bill of Rights. Civil rights in the UK are much more protected by statute law (such as the Human Rights Act) and common law and documents such as Magna Carta. One could argue that Americans' rights are more securely protected, though that constitutional protection is variable: gun owners, for example, are better protected constitutionally than women and children.

The USA has a particular history of minority ethnic groups, especially African-Americans, struggling to achieve equal civil rights. In many ways this is a legacy of slavery and racial segregation in parts of the country thereafter. Certain civil rights issues also have a much higher profile in the US compared with the UK, for example abortion and gun rights.

In the UK, civil rights are often protected by membership of other international bodies, most notably the European Court of Human Rights located in Strasbourg. By contrast, international commitments play no real significant role in the protection of civil rights in America.

In the USA, some civil rights issues have a much more party political and partisan flavour to them. Democrats, for example, are those found predominantly fighting for gay and female reproductive rights while Republicans champion the rights of gun owners and foetuses.

The Supreme Court has played a dominant role in the development and protection of civil rights in the USA, while in the UK that role has more usually been taken by Parliament, for example by passing laws such as the 1975 Sex Discrimination Act and the 2010 Equality Act.

> **Entrenched** Such rights refer to those found in the 1791 Bill of Rights and subsequent constitutional amendments such as the Fourteenth Amendment's Equal Protection clause. They are constitutionally protected from easy change by temporary governments.

Summary

By the end of this section, you should know and understand:

■ How the US Constitution protects civil rights.
■ The other ways in which civil rights have been extended and defended in the USA.
■ The contribution of pressure groups to civil rights.
■ One case study of a civil rights issue and how it has affected US politics.
■ Some of the differences between the USA and the UK in how civil rights are fought for and protected.

You should also be aware of some of the ways that the electoral process and direct democracy impact on other parts of US government and politics. This is known as the **synoptic** element.

■ The role of pressure groups in campaigning for civil rights **(Pressure groups)**.
■ The role of the Supreme Court in the development of civil rights **(The judicial branch of government: the Supreme Court)**.
■ How many civil rights issues help to define US political parties **(Political parties)**.
■ The role of the US Constitution and its amendments in protecting civil rights **(The constitutional frameworks of US government)**.

Questions & Answers

How to approach the Paper 2 exam

This paper is 2 hours long and is divided into three sections, all of which are compulsory. You need to answer **all** the questions in Sections A and B and **one** question in Section C. The format and layout of the paper are the same as those for Papers 1 and 3.

The exam is marked out of 77 and makes up a third of your entire Politics A-level. Your papers on British politics and on political ideas also each represent a third. Section A comprises three short-answer questions, each worth 9 marks, while Sections B and C are both single-answer mini essay-style answers worth 25 marks each. Section B consists of an extract of around 250–300 words from an article (normally recent) about US politics, with a single question based around the ideas contained in the piece. Section C entails a choice between two essay questions requiring a comparison between US and UK politics. You should therefore spend roughly the **same amount of time** on **each section** of the exam. Take particular care not to spend too long on Section A. Allocate 40 minutes maximum, so roughly 12–13 minutes per question. Even if you think you could write more on a single-answer question, don't!

The assessment objectives

The exams measure how students have achieved the following assessment objectives (AOs):

AO1: Demonstrate knowledge and understanding of political institutions, processes, concepts, theories and issues.

AO2: Analyse aspects of politics and political information, including in relation to parallels, connections, similarities and differences.

AO3: Evaluate aspects of politics and political information, including to construct arguments, make substantiated judgements and draw conclusions.

Before the exam

Make sure that you have revised **all** the material in the specification. There is little choice in the exam itself and any topic could be tested in any section of the exam. Therefore you cannot afford to leave out any topic, nor can you leave out the comparative element. Also make sure you have learned all the key concepts and terminology with examples.

Be clear about what skills the examiner is looking for in each section. Section A focuses on AO1 and AO2 so is essentially about displaying your knowledge of the topic and explaining it in a clear and analytical fashion. Section B is more about analysing and reaching your own judgement based on the argument and points in the short extract and is more weighted towards AO2 and AO3. Section C is similarly slanted towards testing your powers of analysis and forming your own conclusions based on accurate knowledge of both political systems.

In the exam room

1   Skim read all the questions first and ideally decide which Section C question you are going to answer.

2   For **Section A**, if the question mentions a specific political concept such as judicial activism, make sure you define it briefly but clearly at the start, before discussing its importance. Make sure you include one or two directly relevant examples to support your answer. Recent examples can be particularly helpful, but are not automatically expected. There is no requirement to make comparisons with the UK in this section. Make sure you refer to *three* distinct ways. You will gain no extra marks for mentioning more than three ways, so do not waste time trying to do so.

3   For **Section B**, spend a few minutes reading through the extract carefully and make sure you understand what its main points are. The question requires you to 'Analyse, evaluate and compare', so make sure you do just that. You will be limited to a maximum of 10/25 marks if your answer makes no reference to the article, no matter how good your essay is. Another key point to remember is that you must make a **judgement** on the various points outlined in the article — which arguments are most convincing and why (citing examples to support your point), which key points, if any, have been left out. You also need to make **synoptic links** to secure high marks: drawing on knowledge from **all** the other parts of your Politics course, both on this paper and on the other two. The topic chosen will largely determine what other relevant links can be made. For example, an extract focused on political parties might well enable you to draw on your knowledge from political ideas. That on the powers of the president invites comparison with the prime minister. Above all, though, make sure synoptic links are brief and relevant.

4   For **Section C**, your essay answer must be directly relevant to the question. Often the question takes the form of a quote, which you then need to analyse and evaluate. So it is probably a good idea right at the start to offer a preliminary judgement as to whether you largely agree or disagree with the statement and offer any qualifications or additional ideas. You must be consistent in your line of analysis, so do not end with a conclusion that is completely different from your introduction. This is why spending 5 minutes or so planning before you start writing is very useful. The essay will always require you to compare directly the British and American political systems, and it is far better to do this throughout your response rather than writing first about one system and then the other and comparing them at the end.

The exam questions in this Student Guide

This Student Guide includes examination-style questions designed to be a key learning, revision and exam preparation resource. Each question is accompanied by a commentary as well as the total number of marks awarded. Use them to help improve your question technique and knowledge.

■ Section A Short-answer questions

The US Constitution

Explain and analyse three ways that the principle of the separation of powers influences US government.

(9 marks)

ⓔ This question tests both knowledge and understanding (AO1). 6 out of 9 marks are available for this skill. It also tests your ability to analyse the material, that is, to explain why it is important in the wider context of US politics (AO2). 3 out of 9 marks are available for this skill. If you identify and explain only two relevant ways, then you will not get more than 6 marks, however good your knowledge and understanding are.

Student A

The separation of powers is very important in the American constitution. It means no one has too much power and power is shared between the president and Congress. ⓐ It is linked in with checks and balances, and also the ideas of Montesquieu. The Supreme Court is also involved. ⓑ No one can serve in more than one branch, for example Hillary Clinton ⓒ. It is unlike the UK where Theresa May is both head of the executive and a member of the legislature. ⓓⓔ

ⓔ **Level 1: 2/9 marks awarded.** ⓐ The student makes a relevant point but fails to develop it sufficiently and refers to only two branches of government. ⓑ While the Supreme Court should form part of the answer, there is no further explanation or analysis. ⓒ While the example could be relevant, no further explanation or knowledge is given — what were her old and new roles, what time period is being referred to here? ⓓ This example is irrelevant as this section of the exam does not require or expect any comparative element with the UK. ⓔ Overall, the answer is weakened by not having three distinct points which are fully explained and developed and it is also very brief.

Student B

The separation of powers is very important to US government for three main reasons. ⓐ Firstly, it means that no one can serve in more than one branch of government. This means, for example, that Joe Biden had to resign as senator for Delaware when Obama tapped him for the post of vice president. However, as president of the Senate, the VP (currently Mike Pence) does have the casting vote in the event of a tie, so it is not a complete separation of powers. ⓑ Secondly, the system often means that there is a competition for power and influence. For example, when one party controls Congress and the president is from the other party there can be a clash of power and wills. For example, the Republican-controlled Congress passed a bill to construct the Keystone XL pipeline in 2015

---

but Democrat president, Obama, vetoed it, meaning that a separation of powers caused gridlock rather than action. c Divided government is common in the USA (e.g. 2012–16) since Congress and the presidency are not elected entirely at the same time. Finally, separation of powers means that the Supreme Court can often prevent laws and government actions from happening by declaring them unconstitutional as they have the power of judicial review. This happened when in 1998 the Court struck down a line item veto law passed by Congress in the ruling *Clinton* v *New York*. d This can mean that the unelected branch of government can impede the wishes of the elected parts. Overall the separation of powers can mean that no one branch has too much power in US government, but in practice it often means that not much gets done! e

e **Level 3: 9/9 marks awarded.** a The student makes a good, clear introduction and sets the scene well for a full development of three points. Note how throughout the answer there is a clear distinction between each of the three points. This makes it much easier for the examiner to give appropriate credit. b This is a good example of a well-informed student going slightly beyond the question and seeing flaws in the simple definition of the term, using a specific example. c This is a good example of analysis as the student clearly and accurately explains a common consequence of the separation of powers. It is also good to see a further explanation for why this is a frequent occurrence in the USA. d This example is relevant and well explained without wasting time going into great detail. e Overall, the answer contains three relevant and distinct factors, each backed up by supporting evidence. There is a wide range of detailed knowledge but also of analysis that explains the implications and outcomes.

Congress

Explain and analyse three ways that the trustee model could be used to study voting behaviour in legislatures.

(9 marks)

e As with the previous question, you are being tested here on knowledge and understanding (AO1). 6 out of 9 marks are available for this skill. You are also being tested on your ability to analyse the material (AO2), where 3 out of 9 marks are available. If you identify and explain only two relevant ways, then you will not get more than 6 marks, however good your knowledge and understanding are. What makes this question slightly more demanding than the previous one, though, is that it requires a comparison between the UK and the USA as well as an understanding of a political concept. In this case it is the trustee model of representation and how it impacts on voting patterns in Congress and in Parliament.

Student A

The trustee model of representation is also known as the Burkean model of representation and is the opposite of the delegate theory. [a] It is relevant and helpful to understanding how MPs/senators vote in both the UK and the USA. In both chambers, legislators will nearly always vote in the best interests of their voters as they see fit. [b] For example, an MP near Heathrow (e.g. Zac Goldsmith) would vote against airport expansion because that is the wish of those he represents. Likewise, a congressman/woman from, say, West Virginia would nearly always vote to support the coal industry and so would be less keen on strict environmental controls. [c] However, sometimes they will vote against the wishes of their constituents in order to be loyal to their party, so they are not always a 'delegate' for their seat/state. For example, some Tory MPs voted for Brexit even though their constituents voted Remain, while some Democrats voted for Obamacare even though their district was 'red' and so against it. [d] The trustee model only explains some of the motives for voting a particular way in the legislature, politics is only local sometimes! [e]

[e] **Level 2: 4/9 marks awarded.** [a] This is a decent start, the student has clearly understood the political concept referred to in the question, but it is rather undeveloped and a bit too brief. [b] Again, this looks promising, a clearly comparative approach is being undertaken, but it is a bit sweeping when referring to 'nearly always'. [c] Again, it is good to see specific examples being cited, but it would be even better if a name was given for the US example and Goldsmith was identified as a former MP. [d] While this is a valid point, there are no specific examples given and the reference to Obamacare and red districts again is rather undeveloped. [e] While this is a fair point, the answer would have benefited from a proper development of three distinct ways in which the trustee model could be used when looking at voting behaviour within legislatures. Overall this is essentially a sound answer to quite a challenging question, especially in the time available. It is generally well focused, is reasonably knowledgeable and is comparative, but above all it does not fully analyse three distinct points.

Student B

The trustee model of representation (otherwise known as the Burkean model) implies that while obviously influenced by the views and wishes of their voters, legislators (MPs and senators/congressmen) will ultimately use their own judgement when deciding how to vote in Congress or Parliament. [a] One way this is useful for studying how legislators vote is to see how frequently they vote against the clear wishes of local voters. Arguably, while it occurs in both countries, it is more prevalent in the UK due to stronger party discipline. [b] While MPs have sometimes rebelled in order to reflect the strongly held views of constituents (e.g. ex Tory MP Zac Goldsmith over Heathrow expansion), many will not, such as some Labour MPs who backed the Iraq War. This can leave them vulnerable at the next election or to deselection by the local party. In the USA, looser party ties and the existence of primaries make this a lot rarer. Thus, several Republican senators from more liberal areas voted in favour of the repeal of DADT, e.g. former senator Mark Kirk from 'blue' Illinois. Meanwhile, 34 Blue Dog Democrats in the House, often from districts that voted Republican for president in 2008, voted against Obamacare. **c** Secondly, the trustee model enables legislators to vote for the national good rather than the narrow local interest. **d** Hence 'pork barrelling', once very common in Congress, was significantly curbed by a moratorium in 2010 because of the amount of wasteful expenditure occurring, despite such projects (e.g. new highways) being popular with the 'folks back home'. Finally, the trustee model enables one to make a very good comparison between the UK and the USA; as previously mentioned, it is stronger in Westminster than in DC. In the USA, legislators are much more likely to see themselves as 'delegates' due to the fear of being primaried or facing hostile 'attack ads' from opponents. **e** These fears often make it difficult for necessary reforms or laws to get through, so gridlock can occur.

e **Level 3: 8/9 marks awarded.** **a** This is an impressive start to the question and displays a clear understanding of the concept of trusteeship and the comparative requirements of the question. **b** The student helpfully identifies their first point clearly and makes a good comparative judgement, which will secure credit for AO2. **c** Here a clear and relevant example is cited to support the point just made. **d** Here, the second point is clearly identified and will again go on to be supported by an example, though this time only from the USA. **e** The third and final point is also made and examples are given, albeit more generally, and the final point is unsubstantiated. It is also good to see a synoptic element here, bringing in knowledge from the electoral process topic. Overall, given the time constraints, this is a cohesive, well-informed and well-focused response. To achieve full marks, the last point needed to be expanded a little, but nonetheless this answer would achieve a top grade.

■ Section B Extract questions

The Supreme Court

ⓔ This extract focuses on the Supreme Court as the guarantor of civil rights for Americans. It requires you not only to understand the main arguments in the passage but also to make an overall judgement on these points. There is scope to bring in wider knowledge from other areas of the course, for example from the US Constitution and the civil rights topic, as well as possibly brief comparison with the UK Supreme Court.

Read the extract below and answer the question that follows. In your answer you should draw on material from across the whole range of your study of Politics.

The Supreme Court and the protection of citizen rights

The sudden death of Justice Antonin Scalia, on 13 February 2016, added a new dimension to the tumultuous US presidential election: the role, influence and direction of the Supreme Court and constitutional law. The passing of Scalia left the court with an even ideological divide. Much commentary on Scalia's successor claimed that the future direction of constitutional law and citizen rights rested on the new justice. But does the court actually perform the role often attributed to it, that of protecting the civil rights and liberties of Americans against government intrusion? Or does Alexander Hamilton's famous description of the court as the 'least dangerous branch' of government apply all too aptly in cases where minority rights confront the popular will of majorities? Many accounts of the Supreme Court relate a seemingly positive story of 'imperial' judges remaking the country's fundamental laws. On this telling, the court sometimes catastrophically failed to stand up for minorities against tyrannical governments by approving certain laws as constitutional. Most infamously, the court upheld racial segregation in *Plessy* v *Ferguson* (1896) and allowed state laws to stand that criminalised consensual gay activities in *Bowers* v *Hardwick* (1986).

Over time, however, the court saw the error of its ways and reversed itself. Overall, the court's record has been a mixed and imperfect one. On issues such as racial, sexual and marriage equality, the court has transformed the landscape of rights permanently. In turn, though, the court has made rulings that limit citizen or group rights. The justices are not isolated individuals. Although they necessarily rule on constitutional law, in so doing they partly reflect what broader society regards as the most fundamental values.

Extract adapted from an article written by Professor Robert Singh for *Politics Review*, November 2016

Analyse, evaluate and compare the arguments in the above passage for and against the Supreme Court as a consistent defender of the civil liberties of US citizens. [25 marks]

Student A

The Supreme Court was set up by the Founding Fathers to defend the entrenched rights of all US citizens, and the protection of 'life, liberty and the pursuit of happiness'. a However, it is debatable whether it has always done this. The article says that sometimes it has but sometimes it has not. b It is all about constitutional law and who is sitting on the Court at the time. In the nineteenth century it supported segregation so did not uphold the rights of African-Americans, but this changed in the 1950s with the verdict in *Brown* v *Topeka* (not mentioned in the article), so now it can be said it does. c It has also sometimes supported the rights of gay Americans (such as recently with equal marriage) but failed to do so in the past, e.g. *Bowers* v *Hardwick*. Because the Court can reverse its decisions, it changes whose rights it defends — white segregationists or black Americans. It has also tried to protect the rights of others not mentioned in the extract, for example gun owners and criminals (Miranda rights), but has also supported the rights of rich individuals and corporations to donate huge amounts of money to candidates — *Citizens United*. d

A lot depends on who is on the Supreme Court. It is now highly politicised and polarised, with justices labelled as either conservatives (e.g. Thomas) or liberals (e.g. Ginsburg). Conservative justices are less interested in protecting the rights of minorities compared with liberal ones. This is why there was so much debate over the vacancy caused by Scalia's death in 2016 as the balance of the Court could be tilted in a liberal direction if Obama had got his nominee, Merrick Garland, through. After his victory in November 2016, Trump had the chance to put forward his own nominee, Neil Gorsuch. e

I think it is true to say that the Court's record has been a 'mixed one' in protecting civil liberties; sometimes they have and sometimes they haven't, it all depends on who the judges are, their judicial philosophy and public opinion. f Arguably the Bill of Rights and not the Supreme Court is the true guarantor of the rights and liberties of US citizens, as it contains the basic freedoms such as First Amendment rights on free speech and the right to a fair trial. The Supreme Court has done a lot (e.g. desegregation) but arguably it could have done a lot more. g Its power of judicial review can be both used and abused. So overall the Supreme Court has largely defended civil liberties and freedoms in the USA, but cannot always be relied upon.

e **Level 2 (top): 10/25 marks awarded.** a The student has got off to a rather worrying start with a factual inaccuracy, having misunderstood the original intention of the Supreme Court and confusing the Declaration of Independence with the Constitution. b Here, the student has understood the basic argument of the extract but the point is barely developed. c While it is good to see outside knowledge brought in, the analysis is rather simplistic and basic. d These two sentences show some intelligent understanding of the argument made in the extract and use relevant own knowledge, but again the detail is rather limited. e Here, the student has rather veered away from the question and has discussed the composition of the Court rather than staying focused on the issue of civil liberties.

[f] The student makes a clear effort here to reach a final judgement, but they do not really refer to the arguments in the extract at all. [g] While the student refers back to the extract (desegregation), there is no suggestion of what the other areas might be. Overall, the answer shows a largely sound if basic comprehension of the extract and some wider knowledge is used relevantly. There are, however, some factual inaccuracies and irrelevant material, and the student makes no real attempt to evaluate the arguments in the passage. Also, few synoptic links are made.

Student B

The Supreme Court has become fundamental to the debate and arguments over the defence of civil liberties and personal freedoms in the USA. Although its original role was rather unclear and limited (hence perhaps Hamilton's comment as 'least dangerous'), [a] through its acquired power of judicial review (*Marbury* v *Madison*) it has become crucial to interpreting the rights and freedoms enshrined in the Constitution, most notably in the Bill of Rights and the amendments passed after the Civil War. [b] The extract argues in a balanced and generally convincing way that the Supreme Court's record is 'mixed and imperfect', focusing mainly on social issues such as gay rights and black civil rights. It is obviously correct to state that the Court can change its mind as it did over segregation (*Plessy* v *Ferguson* was overturned by *Brown* v *Topeka*) and also gay rights (*Bowers* was overturned by *Lawrence* v *Texas*) [c] but it is possibly a bit too optimistic to state categorically that 'the court has transformed the landscape of rights permanently' as any verdict that seems 'moral' now could itself be overturned. [d] As a justice once said, 'The Constitution is what the Supreme Court says it is.' This is one reason why the whole issues of rights and liberties are fluid as attitudes shift over time, both in the Court and among the public at large.

While it is true that the Court can be swayed by broader public opinion, the extract does not really say why or how and sometimes the justices appear to go against public opinion. [e] For example, in the 2010 case *Citizens United* that dealt with campaign finance, most people, including President Obama, disagreed with the verdict. This was a case that defended the rights of rich individuals/corporations to spend unlimited sums in election campaigns provided it was not coordinated with the official campaigns of candidates (Super PACs). So here, the rights of the wealthy were protected but arguably not those of ordinary voters as it gave too much influence to a minority based on a certain 'take' on the First Amendment. This certainly queries the notion of 'consistent defender'. [f]

The passage is correct to note the importance of changing personnel in how it affects the defence of rights and freedoms. The Court is often labelled as liberals versus conservatives, though this is a bit simplistic as Chief Justice Roberts backed Obamacare in the Sibelius case and he is normally viewed as a conservative. Liberal justices are usually loose constructionists who seek to find new rights and meaning in the wording of the Constitution. They are also known as judicial activists, and the Warren Court of the 1960s in particular is renowned for extending civil rights. [g] Examples of 'new' rights discovered by judicial activists include abortion (*Roe* v *Wade*), the right to remain silent when questioned by the police (Miranda rights) and supporting affirmative action. Conservative justices (such as Scalia and Thomas) prefer judicial restraint and believe in a more narrow reading of the Constitution and generally leave civil liberties in the hands of elected legislators. They have, however, found in favour of the rights to individual gun ownership (*DC* v *Heller*) and as mentioned above have defended the rights of the wealthy to make huge political donations. h To see it as a 'consistent defender' of civil liberties would be going too far as so much depends on one's definitions and understanding of rights and freedoms; if you give rights to one group, you very often take them away from another, as the extract implies. It is also not made easier by the vague wording of some phrases in the Constitution, such as 'cruel and unusual punishment'.

Overall it is perhaps fairest to say that different judges have defended the rights of different groups and individuals in US society, partly depending on their own judicial (and sometimes political) outlook, as well as the way the tide of public opinion is flowing. Unlike the UK Supreme Court, i it has played a huge part in shaping the laws of the USA and most major advances in civil liberties are down to landmark cases. This does not automatically mean, though, that it can always defend every individual right all of the time. The extract is correct to see the Court's record as patchy but positive overall.

---

e **Level 5 (mid): 22/25 marks awarded.** a Early on, the student has both referred to a point made in the passage and accurately placed it in context. This suggests the student is well informed and confident; first impressions count. b This section shows both good factual knowledge and an understanding of core concepts (here, judicial review) and also synoptic links with the topic of the US Constitution. c Very good use here of citing wider knowledge (the *Lawrence* case) to support a point made in the extract. d The student has effectively evaluated an argument from the passage by querying the notion of 'permanently', which will gain marks for AO3. e Again, another good example of evaluating an argument in the passage, and the student properly reinforces the point by citing a relevant example, the *Citizens United* case. f This sentence helps to ensure the answer remains focused explicitly on the question and is consistent with previous points made. g This section shows accurate and relevant knowledge of contrasting judicial philosophies, which will gain credit for AO1, but also analyses them in relation to civil liberties, thus also gaining marks for AO2. h This section displays detailed and perceptive knowledge of the complexity of civil liberties and the element of subjectivity. i While it is good to see the synoptic link with the UK, this point might have been better made if it had been included earlier and properly developed; however, it is better to have it here than not mention it at all. Overall, this is a well-structured, coherent and knowledgeable answer. There is excellent understanding of the key arguments made in the passage, but also clear evaluation and judgement. The student makes fully supported and detailed synoptic links, mainly with the US Constitution. Although problematic with the constraints of time, some brief comparison with the UK might have enhanced the answer still further.

Electoral process and direct democracy

ⓔ This extract focuses on some (but not all) of the main arguments for and against the use of ballot propositions in America. Again, it requires you not only to understand the main arguments in the passage but also to make an overall judgement and comparison of these points. There is also scope to bring in wider knowledge from other areas of the course, for example from the Constitution and pressure groups.

Read the extract below and answer the question that follows. In your answer you should draw on material from across the whole range of your study of politics.

Ballot initiatives, or propositions, have a number of advantages. First, they can enable states to pass legislation on controversial matters that state legislatures are unwilling or unable to act upon — these have included: campaign finance reform, term limits and the medical as well as recreational use of marijuana. Secondly, the initiative process can enhance the responsiveness of state legislatures and improve state legislators' performance and accountability. In addition, having propositions, especially high-profile ones, on the ballot can increase overall turnout in November elections. This was the case, for example, in 2004 with a same-sex marriage ban proposition in Ohio which attracted large numbers of conservative Republicans who also voted for President George W. Bush on the same ballot, thus tipping this swing state into the Republican column. Finally, initiatives can increase citizen interest in state issues and encourage other forms of participation in the political process — membership of pressure groups, for example.

There are, however, distinct disadvantages to the process. Propositions by their very nature lack flexibility. Once a measure is drafted, approved and put on the state ballot, it cannot be amended until after it has been passed. So whereas state laws go through a thorough process and can be amended in order to attract wider support or prevent a potential problem in the wording, propositions are set in stone from the start. The proposition process, therefore, lacks the key benefits of the legislative process — debate, compromise, hearings, public input and amendment. Proposition elections are also vulnerable to manipulation by narrow special interest groups — high-spending campaigns and extensive media advertising, especially on television, which is often simplistic and misleading in both language and argument.

Extract taken from an article about US government and politics published in 2013

Analyse, evaluate and compare the arguments in the above passage for and against the use of propositions in the USA.

(25 marks)

Student A

There are many arguments for and against ballot initiatives (also known as propositions) which are one of the main forms of direct democracy in the USA but only at a state level. The other types are recall elections and referendums. Some but not all of the main ones are mentioned in the extract. In favour of propositions is the fact that initiatives can deal with controversial issues such as legalising marijuana (e.g. Colorado 2012), it also makes state politicians more accountable, and improves turnout. Finally it can help political participation as voters will be more likely to join pressure groups if they support or propose a ballot initiative measure that they care deeply about, such as gay marriage or abortion. **a**

However, there are also a number of problems correctly identified in the extract. A proposition is a bit of a 'blunt instrument', it cannot be amended or changed. So you either allow the sale of marijuana or not. **b** There is also the problem of special interests and powerful pressure groups such as the NRA or the Mormon Church that spent $20 million on backing Prop 8 in California to ban same-sex marriage. **c** Arguably, direct democracy is just as dependent and manipulated by the powerful and wealthy as indirect democracy.

There are, though, arguments on both sides not mentioned in the passage. **d** For example, in support of propositions it could be said that they act as a 'legislative laboratory'. A law begins in a single state and then spreads across the States if it is seen to work. Also, it does enable ordinary voters to draw up rules and laws that they really care about, and not just those passed by the political elites. **e** The USA does not, however, have national referendums/direct democracy like the UK — Brexit vote and Scottish independence. Also, congressmen cannot be recalled, only state-level officials. One argument against initiatives not mentioned in the passage is how they add to the overall (and already huge) cost of American politics. For example, in 2016, around $1 billion was spent on ballot initiative campaigns, with $128 million being spent in California alone on Prop 61 that was to do with drug prices. **f**

Overall I would argue that the points in favour of ballot initiatives are stronger than those against. It is after all the 'purest form' of democracy and is popular with many voters, and also allows voters to set some of the political agenda and make their views known. Yes, it is not perfect and there are important and relevant flaws to the system, but it does provide a check and balance to state governments, which is after all a key principle of US politics. **g**

---

e **Level 3 (low): 12/25 marks awarded.** **a** This is a sound introduction which shows the student has correctly identified and understood the main points in the extract, and introduces an accurate example from wider knowledge, namely marijuana legalisation. However, there is no hint of evaluation or comparison of arguments, which will limit marks, especially for AO3. There is also no need to list the other forms of direct democracy. **b** While the student makes an attempt at evaluating an argument, the example they have chosen is arguably not the best; legalising marijuana could be said to be an area where legislative precision would prove very helpful. **c** While it is good to see a detailed and relevant example here with reference to the Mormon Church, the NRA example is not developed at all, which makes it less convincing. **d** While it is good to bring in wider knowledge and describing omissions does constitute some evaluation of the passage, it would be better if this type of point was incorporated into a more general evaluation of the extract. **e** Here the student makes two valid points, but they give no examples, which limits the marks that can be awarded for AO1 and AO2. **f** Again, the student offers a good point, with some evidence, but it would have been even better if they had given more explanation. **g** The conclusion is reasonably satisfactory and is at least focused on the question. There is also a somewhat general evaluation and comparison of the key points in the passage, and a hint of synopticity at the very end when the student refers to checks and balances. It is a pity, though, that they did not introduce this earlier in the answer. Overall this is a moderate answer. The student clearly has some knowledge of the topic, the examples they provide are relevant and accurate, and they have clearly understood the passage. What lets it down is the fairly limited depth of knowledge and range of examples, and perhaps most importantly, the absence of any really convincing analysis or evaluation of the arguments in the extract.

Student B

There are many points both for and against the use (in many but not all states) of ballot initiatives. Some of the key ones on both sides are identified in the extract, though not all. **a** Firstly, it is fair comment to say that propositions often act as a 'blunt instrument' and cannot be amended or altered by state governments. This can lead to unintended consequences, such as someone being jailed for life for stealing a pizza as a result of the 'three strikes' laws that were passed in many states (around 30) from the 1990s. **b** This is especially convincing as an argument when dealing with complex issues such as legalising the sale of marijuana where expert knowledge and carefully crafted legislation is probably necessary. However, in some cases it can work well enough; for example, same-sex marriage is essentially a binary issue, one is either for or against it. **c** In addition, as the extract usefully explains, it does ensure that laws on important matters actually get passed. State governments (there is no federal direct democracy provision in the USA, unlike the UK with the Brexit vote) can be equally as reluctant and slow to pass laws as Congress. Governors have the power of veto, and there can often be divided control of bicameral state legislatures, so gridlock ensues. While the passage refers to 'compromise', that is often rarely the case in modern and highly polarised US politics, even at state level. Direct democracy is able to bypass this potential logjam. **d** Also, it is somewhat contradictory to note on the one hand a lack of debate about issues and then subsequently to refer to 'media blitzes'. Debates in state legislatures are not necessarily any more objective than partisan ads on TV or in the media.

It is also a valid argument that turnout and political participation can be improved by ballot initiatives. It is true that Bush was helped to win Ohio in 2004 by Rove's strategy of 'getting out the vote', but it should be noted that he had also won the state in 2000 without a high-profile proposition on the ballot, and the same could be said for Trump in 2016. **e** Arguably, turnout can equally be depressed by ballot initiatives as it can lead to 'voter fatigue' with too many issues on the ballot. For example, in 2016 voters in California as well as voting for president and Congress had ballots on issues ranging from the death penalty to the use of condoms in porn movies. This particular argument is therefore not entirely convincing. f

Perhaps the biggest weakness identified by the passage is how most ballots are organised and funded by wealthy individuals or special interest groups. The cost of campaigning for ballot propositions often runs into millions of dollars; around $1 billion was spent in 2016 alone. Voters are besieged with ads which often confuse rather than inform them. For example, in the campaign over Prop 8 in California in 2008 (anti gay marriage), opponents argued in TV ads that it would impose religious beliefs on citizens and give the state too much power into people's private lives. g Not mentioned in the passage but very relevant is the cost of just getting a measure onto the ballot. For example, nearly 370,000 signatures are required just to get a proposed law on the ballot in California. This alone takes a lot of time, money and resources, so many organisers employ professional petition consultants, such as APC. This arguably is one of the strongest arguments against the use of ballot initiatives as it means that they are not really 'pure democracy' but more the 'politics of the purse', a criticism that is also frequently levelled at indirect democracy. In 2016, a California ballot initiative on drug price reform was defeated in part due to huge donations by major drug firms such as Pfizer. A rather weaker argument is that the accountability of local politicians is enhanced; this is probably truer of another form of direct democracy, namely recall elections. h Some might say that the whole notion of direct democracy undermines (and at worst stifles) representative government where representatives are trusted to make their own decisions on issues and are held accountable every two or four years at election time.

Overall, the passage makes for a useful if somewhat incomplete analysis of the strengths and weaknesses of one aspect of direct democracy in the USA. Arguably, the main weakness (that of cost and complexity) is only partially explained, but it is correct to state that often but not always they can be a blunt instrument. Less convincing are the points about improving turnout and accountability. i

e **Level 5 (high): 24/25 marks awarded.** a As with Student B in the previous sample answer, the student gives a clear and crisp introduction; this sets up the scene well. b This is a very good example of making a valid point and supporting it with relevant and factual own knowledge. The student intelligently amplifies and develops upon the basic point made in the passage. c Here, the student makes effective use of the balanced argument; they agree with some aspects of the point made in the passage, but their answer also intelligently counters it by using an opposing example, namely equal marriage. This will gain credit for both AO1 and AO2. d This part of the answer demonstrates some excellent evaluation and judgement (AO3) and also displays accurate knowledge of how state-level government can work; there is an element of synoptic knowledge about Congress, too. It is good that the student then goes on to explore an apparent contradiction in the passage over debate and publicity. e The student makes excellent use of own knowledge here to query a point made in the article. The references to 2000 and 2016 suggest an extremely well-informed student so secure credit for both AO1 and AO3. ⓕ This ending to the paragraph works well as it shows both detailed and up-to-date knowledge, and remains clearly focused on the question, making a convincing comment about the extract. ⓖ The student makes good use here of a point that they then fully develop with examples. ⓗ Here the student gives a clearly set out evaluation of an argument made in the passage, and the point about recall elections is especially insightful and relevant. ⓘ This is a good brief overview of the preceding points which very much focuses on both analysing and comparing the arguments in the passage. Overall this is a high-quality answer. It is clear, coherent and well set out. There are plenty of examples of relevant detailed knowledge, and also consistent evaluation rather than the student just repeating uncritically the points raised in the extract.

■ Section C Comparative essay question

Comparing political parties in the USA and the UK

'Political parties are more democratic in America than the UK.' Analyse and evaluate this statement. In your answer you should draw on material from across the whole range of your course of study in politics.

(25 marks)

ⓔ This question requires knowledge of the operation and organisation of the main political parties in both countries, and a discussion of the notion of democracy. It also offers opportunities for synoptic links to areas such as voter turnout and the respective powers of the president and the prime minister in their roles as party leaders.

Student A

Political parties are very important to all democracies, they enable voters to participate and make informed choices. ⓐ They help them decide between different ideologies (e.g. socialist for the UK Labour Party and conservative for the US Republican Party) and different policies such as free healthcare and reducing the scale of cuts in welfare benefits. ⓑ They are both democratic because the members/supporters choose the leaders, and even sometimes the candidates, though this is truer for the USA, but some would say that neither system is fully democratic and each has its flaws. Overall I largely agree with the statement, but UK parties can be democratic too.

The US party system is more democratic because of primaries and caucuses. Every four years, supporters get to choose the presidential candidate for the two main parties, Democrat and Republican. In 2016 the Republicans chose Donald Trump while the Democrats selected Hillary Clinton. Trump went on to win the presidential election in November. ⓒ Primaries and caucuses allow ordinary voters to choose rather than just party activists in 'smoke-filled rooms', as was often the case before 1968. Some states, mostly larger ones such as Florida and New York, hold primaries, which are secret ballots. Smaller states, most infamously Iowa, use caucuses, which are more informal and take longer. Although nearly anyone can vote in these contests, not many do, so perhaps they aren't all that democratic! Also, a lot of time and money is spent on attacking other candidates from the same party. ⓓ For example, Trump referred to 'Lying Ted' and 'Cry Baby Rubio', which is not really very democratic as it makes it all about personalities, not policies. Also policies are decided by the candidates, not the voters. Many Republicans do not want a wall along the border with Mexico, but Trump does, so he will work hard to ensure it happens. There are also lots of rich donors and wealthy pressure groups in the USA who give money to candidates, which makes them less democratic. There are better laws in the UK that prevent this abuse of power from happening. ⓔ

The UK party system is less democratic because it generally involves far fewer people. Groups such as the National Trust and the RSPB have many more members than either the Labour or Conservative parties. Only party members can vote on policies and leadership, and even then they often don't have a say. For example, in 2015 Theresa May became Tory PM without anyone other than her MPs having a say. ⒤ This is not very democratic, although Cameron was chosen by the party members over David Davis a few years ago. Labour is arguably more democratic as Jeremy Corbyn has now been elected twice as leader (in 2015 and 2016) even if he has fallen out with most of his MPs, e.g. Tristan Hunt. Party members can also have a say in policies and manifestos, though less so than in the past, e.g. Labour Party conferences. Only party members can choose or even de-select their local candidates, this means real power only lies with the 'core'. Also, all candidates have to be approved by the national party and sometimes women can be imposed on a constituency (all-women shortlists). I don't think anyone in the national Republican Party would have approved of Trump! ⒢

Overall, both political systems have bits of democracy in their parties, but the USA has more, mainly because of primaries. UK parties are too dominated by a small group of party activists and also, in Labour, by the trade unions, which provide most of the funding, e.g. Unite union. ⒣

ⓔ **Level 2 (top): 10/25 marks awarded.** ⒜ The student appears to have somewhat misunderstood the reference to the term 'democracy', so not a good start, though the rest of the answer suggests that they did understand the main thrust of the question. ⒝ While it is good to use examples, those chosen here are rather vague and unclear — which parties/countries is the answer referring to? ⒞ This is a classic example of throwing in a fact for its own sake. The question does not require knowledge of the outcome of the 2016 election. ⒟ While the points made in this section are relevant, they are weakened by lack of examples. A rough figure for primaries and caucuses turnout would be helpful, as would a precise example of a figure regarding expenditure. In addition, the point about voter eligibility is very loosely phrased; a top-level student would be far more precise, referring to closed/open primaries, etc. ⒠ The previous two sentences, although making valid points, again lack proper details or examples and the final point is not developed at all — what, briefly, are the laws regarding election finance in the UK? ⒤ Again, while this is factually correct and relevant, there is no real depth of knowledge about May's election, e.g. Andrea Leadsom dropping out of the final round. ⒢ While this view might be true and the general point has some validity, beware of making throwaway and generalised comments like this without developing them properly. ⒣ Again, while a relevant point, never include new material in a conclusion. The point about trade union funding and Labour should be made earlier on, and also could have been used very effectively to compare with political funding in the USA, suggesting that neither system is entirely without its dependence on special interests. Overall, this is a brief essay that has some relevance to the question, shows knowledge with some relevant examples and makes a basic conclusion. It lacks the real depth and mastery of detail to score higher than a C/D grade.

Student B

Political parties are a fundamental part of any modern democracy, but more debatable is how democratic the parties are themselves. On the surface there is a lot of evidence to support the view that US parties are more democratic than those in the UK, but in reality there is also a case to be made that the statement is too simplistic. The best way to evaluate this interpretation is to compare how candidates are selected, how policies are decided and how the parties are financed. a

When assessing candidate selection, the US system appears the more democratic due to the widespread use of party primaries, and to a lesser extent caucuses. b Participation in primaries is open to a wide range of voters, though this varies a little state by state, with some having open primaries and others having closed or semi-closed ones. California has what is known as a jungle primary. In essence, anyone who is registered as either a Democrat or Republican (or indeed of a third party such as the Libertarians) can vote in that party's primary to help choose candidates. c This is particularly important for the presidential election when, for example, in 2016 the Republicans chose Trump over rivals such as Cruz and Kasich, while Hillary Clinton defeated Bernie Sanders in the Democratic race. But voters can also choose candidates for lesser offices, such as Congress, and can even 'de-select' the incumbent (e.g. Eric Cantor in Virginia, a senior House Republican). This is much more democratic than the 'smoke-filled rooms' where party bosses made all the decisions. By contrast, in the UK it is normally only party members who get to choose the leader and local candidates. With falling party memberships (the Conservatives used to have around 3 million members in the 1950s but have only around 150,000 today), d this is hardly as democratic as letting all supporters of the party have a say. Labour did, however, offer a supporter category of membership at £5, which enabled one to have a vote in the leadership election. Also, Theresa May was not even elected by the party membership as her final rival, Andrea Leadsom, dropped out of the contest before the vote went to the members. Gordon Brown was also 'crowned' leader after Tony Blair resigned in 2007.

But even in the USA, it is not all that democratic. Turnout is often very low in primaries and more so in caucuses. Even the first and often critical Iowa caucus only saw 16% of voters turn out in 2016. e Also there have been some attempts to introduce primary-style elections by the Conservatives, for example in Totnes, after the MP expenses scandal. Also the cost and length of presidential primaries in the USA means that successful candidates either have to be wealthy personally (e.g. Trump) or attract a lot of wealthy donors. Arguably this does not promote true democracy in parties. f

When it comes to policy making, it could be said that neither system is particularly democratic as the leader/winning candidate has a lot of freedom to choose his/her own policies, especially in the USA. In the UK, party policy is often debated at the annual conferences, and in the Labour Party, conference used to have a lot of power in this area, but much less so nowadays as it was seen as too divisive. g The Conservative Party has always deferred to its leader — for example, David Cameron decided to push through gay marriage as PM despite it not being in the 2010 manifesto or supported/debated at conference. Likewise, presidents can largely decide their own policies once selected, though they would be very wise to honour previous pledges such as building a wall with Mexico and implementing a travel ban on many Muslims (Trump), and introducing healthcare and immigration reforms (Obama). As parties are much weaker in the USA and the system is much more candidate focused, parties have relatively little say formally in the formation of policy. Therefore neither party system is particularly democratic when it comes to policy making, but perhaps that is understandable given the need to be flexible to events and the fact that the 'core' (those most likely to vote in primaries or join a political party in the first place) are likely to be more extreme in their views than the average voter. Many Labour activists, for example, would like to see widespread nationalisation and other core socialist policies such as major wealth redistribution, while many of the Republican core would like abortion banned completely. h

Party funding is also an area where neither party system is more democratic than the other. In fact, the USA is probably less democratic than the UK in this regard. A great deal of power and influence lies with rich individuals and powerful pressure groups who help to bankroll much of US politics. Wealthy donors such as the Koch Brothers and Sheldon Adelson wield a lot of influence via their political donations. For example, in 2012, one of the Koch brothers gave $1 million to the pro-Romney Super PAC, Restore Our Future. Pressure groups such as the NRA and the Human Rights Campaign (a pro-LGBT advocacy group) i also play a major role in campaign finance and lobbying parties and their candidates, through their PACs. Attempts to reform campaign finance have been very difficult (especially after *Citizens United*) j so money is an ever-growing issue in US politics and therefore parties, and one that undermines democracy, as those with the 'biggest bucks' have the loudest voice. The UK has more restrictive laws on campaign and party finance but there is still evidence of some corruption and democratic failings. For example, many have argued the trade unions affiliated to Labour, such as Unite led by Len McCluskey, have too much power and influence. The same could be true of wealthy individual donors who often end up with peerages in return for large donations, for example Tory peer Lord Farmer had previously donated £6.5 million before receiving his peerage in 2014.

In conclusion, while US parties can appear more democratic due mainly to primaries and caucuses, both systems have opportunities for democratic participation, but both are also subject to undue influence from wealthy donors and special interests. Perhaps it would be fairer to say US parties are weaker but slightly more democratic. k

e **Level 5: 23/25 marks awarded. a** This introduction works very well. It is clearly focused on the question, suggests a nuanced answer is most accurate, and also sets out three clear and relevant themes by which the statement can be evaluated. This will enable the student to have thematic sections where they can compare and contrast the UK and US party systems. **b** The first sentence of this paragraph identifies the main focus, namely primaries and caucuses, and makes an accurate preliminary judgement. It therefore provides a good starting point for further development of the argument backed up by examples. **c** The student clearly has detailed and accurate knowledge of the variations within the primary system, but their answer might have been even better if they had given examples of open and closed primaries. They do define (briefly) a jungle primary. Mention of the Libertarian Party is also welcome and relevant — unexpected but entirely creditworthy. **d** The student offers clear, precise and accurate use of knowledge here to support a point which they then develop and link in directly to the question. Sensibly they choose only one example from UK politics to illustrate their point as time pressure makes any more problematic.

e A good counterpoint is made regarding primaries, and citing a recent relevant example from the UK enhances the quality of the answer. **f** It is helpful to return explicitly to the original question at the end of a paragraph, but it would have been even better if the argument was developed slightly more, for example by explaining the dangers money and wealth pose to democracy and political parties, though this theme is addressed in more detail later on. **g** The student makes a good point here, but arguably it is still a little too vague — an example of divisiveness would have helped. **h** These last two sentences work very well — there are relevant examples from both systems, and the point is fully developed. There is also a brief nod to the student's study of political ideas and a key notion of socialist ideology. A good synoptic link has been made. **i** The student cites two good and contrasting examples; one is perhaps obvious and very well known, the NRA, the other less so. There is nothing wrong in using well-trodden examples, but there should also be evidence of the less well-known but equally relevant examples. **j** Another good use of a synoptic link, this time with the judiciary.

k The conclusion is rather short, but given time constraints and the overall length of the response, this is fine. It is clearly focused on the question and also neatly reworks the original statement into a more accurate final judgement entirely consistent with the preceding argument. Overall, while this is not a perfect essay, in the time available it is a full, focused, well-organised and coherent response. Examples are numerous, accurate and well deployed. Good synoptic links are often made as well. This would receive a high A grade.

Knowledge check answers

1 The president is checked by Congress, which can overturn his veto with a supermajority, reject his appointments (Senate only) and ultimately impeach him, and by the Supreme Court, which can declare his actions unconstitutional. Congress is checked by the president, who can veto bills, and by the Supreme Court, which again can declare laws unconstitutional. The Supreme Court can be checked by the president, who makes appointments to the court and can, with the consent of Senate, increase its overall size — court-packing. It can also be checked by Congress, which can pass constitutional amendments again with a supermajority.

2 The organisation of elections such as direct democracy and primaries rests with states, as does the death penalty and the power to levy local taxes such as a sales tax. Federal government oversees all foreign policy, levies a federal income tax and manages certain national programmes, such as Medicare and Medicaid, though often working alongside state governments.

3 The Founding Fathers wanted a constitution that had a degree of permanence and stability based around shared common values and principles such as republican government and checks and balances.

4 In essence, because this is how the US Constitution has evolved and developed since the eighteenth century. With formal amendment being difficult to achieve, informal amendment has enabled it to keep up to date relatively easily even if controversy often ensues.

5 All states are allocated two senators each, regardless of population size, but their allocation of House members depends on population numbers, which are reviewed every ten years following the national census, a process known as reapportionment.

6 There are a number of reasons. One is that bills have become longer and more complex. The average length for bills in 1948 was two and a half pages; it is now over 20. Yet some bills are even longer — the Affordable Care Act, for example, ran to 2400 pages. Also, the recent and rapid decline in pork-barrelling (favoured special projects of law-makers) has meant that Congress is now less inclined to pass bills about which it has reservations as there is no longer any quid pro quo. There is also the little matter of hyper-partisanship, which makes consensus harder to achieve, and increased use of the filibuster in the Senate.

7 Members of Congress remain older, whiter, more male and also considerably richer and better educated than the average US citizen. The most glaring anomaly is perhaps how much more religious they are.

8 Party whips do not have the same incentives to offer, such as promotion to ministerial office, as whips in Westminster do. They are also aware that members of Congress need to prioritise their own re-election chances and of the need to keep in with the party 'core' in their state or district. Their relative weakness reflects the looser party organisation still evident in Congress.

9 In many ways it depends on what you mean by powerful. When one party controls both houses and the White House, then Congress can pass many laws that reflect their party's agenda. Equally, when there is divided government, Congress is powerful (or frustrating!) in that it can effectively thwart much of the president's legislative programme, especially the more controversial aspects, forcing him to use other, less effective means, such as executive orders, to achieve his aims.

10 The variable factors on presidential power include the stage of the presidential term (honeymoon or lame-duck period?), their personal poll ratings, whether their party controls Congress or not and the nature of the issue: presidents have much more leeway in foreign affairs as opposed to domestic policy.

11 'Insider' presidents will know from the start 'how Washington works' and the 'levers' to pull. They will also probably already have close contacts in Congress, especially from their own party.

12 There is no single answer as to when a US president is strongest, but probably the potential is greatest at a time of national crisis, especially external, when the public look to them for leadership and Congress is less likely to be difficult. For example, Bush Jr managed to get the Patriot Act passed swiftly after 9/11.

13 Most presidencies could be said ultimately to be failures due in part to the high expectations placed upon them, which is of course a necessity in getting elected in the first place. They overpromise and inevitably under-deliver. Most offer hope and change when in fact there are usually so many restrictions on their power that disappointment is built in. For instance, a strong foreign policy usually requires higher levels of defence spending, which in turn makes tax cuts or greater spending on social programmes all the harder. As President Johnson so eloquently put it, 'They geld us first and then expect us to win the Kentucky Derby.'

14 It is fairest to say that Supreme Court justices have to pass a judicial capability threshold, but selection then takes place according to their perceived judicial and indeed political bias. Presidents tend to look for justices 'in their own image'. The president's legal team undertakes extensive research on past judgements and published comments to ensure this happens and the appointee does not 'disappoint'.

Knowledge check answers

15 Judicial review is the most important power of the Court. It involves assessing whether or not an action or law is unconstitutional. If the former, then it can be 'struck down'. This power reflects the Court's ability to interpret the Constitution.

16 Republicans prefer strict constructionists as a rule because they are less likely to 'discover' new rights in the Constitution for causes they disapprove of, such as LGBT rights. They also tend to prefer states' rights over and above a powerful federal government. There is an element of hypocrisy here, however — few Republicans would be content to see Democrat-run states impose strict gun control laws within their own states.

17 Landmark judgements refer to cases that have a lasting significance and impact in a contentious area such as abortion, race or gun laws. In reality, the majority of cases before the Supreme Court are much less high profile and consequently receive much less attention.

18 All of the House and a third of the Senate are elected. The mid-terms can often therefore result in a shift in control of Congress, normally away from the president's party. Many governors and state government posts are also elected at this time.

19 Primaries and caucuses remind us that the actual conduct of elections is left to individual states. There is therefore considerable variety and difference between them. Each state has its own laws (along with local party rules) that determine the exact nature of these elections, such as who can vote — closed or open primaries, or variations of both. The same variety also applies to direct democracy in the USA.

20 If there was no clear winner with an overall majority of delegates by the end of the primaries/caucuses process, the convention would then become the forum for deal-making between delegates and candidates, with further stages of voting until an outright winner emerged. In reality, though, the parties would do all they could to try to avoid this scenario, which would accentuate divisions within the party.

21 In short, because the current system preserves their cosy duopoly. Any system of awarding electors proportionally by state would not only increase the possibility of no one candidate winning the Electoral College outright but could also encourage more voters to vote for third-party and independent candidates in the first place. As it stands, the Electoral College offers both main parties a decent chance of winning the presidency. No party has won the presidency more than three times in a row since the 1940s.

22 Televised debates have relatively little impact on the final result normally because both candidates prepare thoroughly for them, often being coached for likely questions. Even if the first debate goes unexpectedly poorly, as did Obama's in 2012, they usually come back stronger in the subsequent showdowns. With so much potentially at stake, both sides tend to be largely defensive in their approach and take few risks.

23 The failure to reform campaign finance effectively rests largely with the current Supreme Court. It is very much the Court's interpretation of the First Amendment that has handicapped legislation such as BCRA. There is no obligation to ascribe to corporations First amendment rights or to see political donations as a vital part of free political expression.

24 In strict legal terms, measures passed via direct democracy have no more power than other state laws. The nature of their mandate, though, does act as a strong disincentive for state legislatures to overturn such measures by law, at least in the short term, as they would be seen to be blatantly disregarding the clearly expressed views of their voters.

25 There are a number of reasons. Many of the Democrat policies, such as a pro-choice platform, play well with these groups. Also, their Republican opponents are often portrayed as being more hostile to embracing their causes. Wider social movements such as feminism and black civil rights have historic links with the more socially progressive of the two parties. This was especially true after much of the conservative southern (and segregationist) Democrats were alienated from their national leadership by the passage of civil rights laws in the 1960s. The more hawkish and pro-gun stance of many Republicans also puts off many black and female voters.

26 Clinton won the popular vote by a clear margin but lost decisively in the Electoral College. This was primarily due to the distribution of her votes — she piled up huge numbers of votes in well-populated 'blue' states such as New York and California but narrowly lost the vote in a number of crucial swing states such as Ohio, with the result that all their ECV went to Donald Trump. Many political commentators have noted how the Democrat vote is heavily concentrated in a few core states on each coastline but is thinner elsewhere. The Republican vote, by contrast, is distributed more equally across a wider number of states.

27 Congress is more likely to be composed of strong partisans on both sides. When voters split their ticket more frequently, they often plumped for more moderate congressional candidates from either party. Nowadays, it is much more likely that legislators represent districts/states that are blue or red. Fewer moderates also means compromise is harder to achieve in Congress. In summary, it has both contributed to and reflects higher levels of partisanship.

28 Political advertising in the USA is much more accessible (and also more costly) than in the UK. There are no really effective laws regulating the number or frequency of political ads, with the result that airwaves, especially in swing states, are inundated with such adverts. Single 30-second ads can cost thousands of dollars on primetime TV slots. Such an advertising blitz would be impossible legally in the UK where parties are tightly limited to the number of (free) party election broadcasts they can air.

29 The central party structures have only a limited amount of power. Most candidates raise their own campaign funds and conduct their election bids themselves. The national committees can channel some central funding into competitive congressional races where a strong candidate could need additional help to 'get them over the line'. Endorsements from senior party figures can also prove useful.

30 'Purple America' is the term used to describe those parts of the USA that are not strongly 'red' or 'blue' but are competitive for both parties. It covers both swing states and individual districts that could go either way. Given the propensity even for safe states to elect state-level officials from the other party on occasion, some might argue that America is more purple than it appears at first glance.

31 The biggest change would be a move to more proportional election systems for both congressional and presidential elections. In addition, changes to the eligibility requirements for the televised TV debates and to ballot access laws could benefit third-party and independent candidates.

32 Pressure groups can endorse favoured candidates and even make campaign donations via PACs. They can air TV ads either supporting or, more usually, attacking individual candidates. And they can publish information on candidates' relevant voting records/ public stances.

33 Members of Congress are subject to a number of influences when it comes to casting their votes. While pressure groups clearly wield some influence, not least through political donations and endorsements, legislators also need to pay close attention to the views of their voters and, to a lesser extent, their party leadership. In any case, most pressure groups donate to candidates already sympathetic to their aims. Money does not directly buy votes but it does help considerably with access.

34 Incumbents receive disproportionately more in donations from pressure groups for the simple reason that many groups prefer to back winners, seeing this as the best way to secure a degree of access to legislators. With money still an important ingredient in electoral success, better-funded candidates are more likely to get elected in the first place — and to stay elected.

35 Pressure groups often have large memberships; the labour organisation AFL-CIO has 12.5 million members while the American Association of Retired Persons (AARP) has around 35 million. In addition, their methods of campaigning, including marches, encouraging mass lobbying of congressmen, etc., can involve a wider range of citizens than those who traditionally get involved in election campaigns. Note, however, that mass participation does not always equate to success. Some of the most powerful pressure groups have a smaller but very influential membership.

36 There are two fundamental reasons based around the Constitution. First, its federal nature means that power is shared between the federal government in DC and the individual states. Second, the system of checks and balances and separation of powers means that power at the centre is also dispersed, with different bodies (Congress, federal bureaucracy, etc.) all having an input into policy making.

37 Civil rights have been extended in a number of ways: by formal constitutional amendments such as granting women the right to vote, by Supreme Court judgements that have 'found' new rights in the Constitution and by federal laws. Pressure groups have also been important in bringing pressure to bear on the courts, Congress and the president to extend rights for those they represent.

Index

Note: **bold** page numbers indicate where definitions of key terms are to be found.

Index